UNDERSTANDING FRANCISCO GOLDMAN

UNDERSTANDING CONTEMPORARY AMERICAN LITERATURE

Matthew J. Bruccoli, Founding Editor

Linda Wagner-Martin, Series Editor

UNDERSTANDING

FRANCISCO GOLDMAN

Ariana E. Vigil

The University of South Carolina Press

Published by the University of South Carolina Press
Columbia, South Carolina 29208

www.sc.edu/uscpress

Manufactured in the United States of America

27 26 25 24 23 22 21 20 19 18
10 9 8 7 6 5 4 3 2 1

Library of Congress Cataloging-in-Publication Data
can be found at http://catalog.loc.gov/.

ISBN 978-1-61117-920-0 (hardback)
ISBN 978-1-61117-921-7 (ebook)

This book was printed on recycled paper with
30 percent postconsumer waste content.

CONTENTS

SERIES EDITOR'S PREFACE

The Understanding Contemporary American Literature series was founded by the estimable Matthew J. Bruccoli (1931–2008), who envisioned these volumes as guides or companions for students as well as good nonacademic readers, a legacy that will continue as new volumes are developed to fill in gaps among the nearly one hundred series volumes published to date and to embrace a host of new writers only now making their marks on our literature.

As Professor Bruccoli explained in his preface to the volumes he edited, because much influential contemporary literature makes special demands, "the word *understanding* in the titles was chosen deliberately. Many willing readers lack an adequate understanding of how contemporary literature works; that is, of what the author is attempting to express and the means by which it is conveyed." Aimed at fostering this understanding of good literature and good writers, the criticism and analysis in the series provide instruction in how to read certain contemporary writers—explicating their material, language, structures, themes, and perspectives—and facilitate a more profitable experience of the works under discussion.

In the twenty-first century Professor Bruccoli's prescience gives us an avenue to publish expert critiques of significant contemporary American writing. The series continues to map the literary landscape and to provide both instruction and enjoyment. Future volumes will seek to introduce new voices alongside canonized favorites, to chronicle the changing literature of our times, and to remain, as Professor Bruccoli conceived, contemporary in the best sense of the word.

Linda Wagner-Martin, Series Editor

ACKNOWLEDGMENTS

My first thanks go to Francisco Goldman, whose prose I have long admired. His novels offer engrossing narratives that touch on some of the most important issues of our time while the characters he creates are memorable and human. His most recent nonfiction writings, particularly those stemming from and dealing with Mexico, offer the kind of insider's perspective that so many of us living in the United States but with deep ties to Latin America find resonant. And, as a binational writer, he has a voice and perspective that make space for those of us, like myself, who are children of several diasporas. Thank you to Jennifer Ho for alerting me to the opportunity to write this book and to Linda Wagner-Martin and Jim Denton for their interest in this project and assistance with bringing the manuscript to print. Thanks to Jennifer Harford Vargas for reading drafts of several chapters and offering astute feedback and to Jes Boon for looking into some of the references in *The Divine Husband* and offering her opinion on seventeenth-century Spanish Catholicism. A second thank-you to Jennifer Ho, a longtime friend, mentor, and colleague, for always being willing to share ideas, listen to problems, and offer advice on any subject personal, political, or academic. Thank you Mario Morales for reintroducing me to D.F., for your warmth, humor, and hospitality, and Alejandra Márquez for your shared love of the city and for reading and discussing the last chapters of the manuscript. Research support was provided by the University of North Carolina–Chapel Hill. Finally, thank you to my family, especially my father, David Vigil, who always offers support and sincere engagement with my work.

CHAPTER 1

Understanding Francisco Goldman

Within Latina/o communities in the United States, it is not uncommon to hear criticisms of those who refer to the United States as "America." America, we should keep in mind, is not synonymous with the United States of America but rather includes two continents and dozens of countries. And yet, even cognizant of this dual reference of the word "America," Francisco Goldman is a truly American writer. Goldman's work spans countries, continents, languages, and time periods. He has made use of a wide variety of genres; some, such as the novel, are widely familiar to U.S. audiences, while others, like the *crónica* (chronicle), are more well known within a Latin American context. While moving seamlessly between different styles and locations, his writing remains grounded in stories of the human condition—including the love, political intrigue, search for belonging, and quest for justice—that have spurred centuries of literature.

Goldman's expansive literary career can be linked to his binational childhood. He was born in Boston, Massachusetts, in 1954, the son of a Catholic Guatemalan mother and Jewish American father. His mother is *mestiza,* a term that denotes a racial or ethnic mix between those indigenous to the Western Hemisphere and their European conquerors. The same idea is expressed by the word *ladino* in Guatemala, and that term is also used to distinguish between this population and indigenous Guatemalans, particularly those who wear traditional *traje* (clothing) and speak an indigenous language, and who make up 60 percent of that country's population. According to the author, his family's background is similar to that of Rogerio Graetz, the protagonist of his first novel, *The Long Night of White Chickens.* Like Goldman, Graetz is the son of a working-class Jewish American father from Boston and a middle-class mother from Guatemala. However, Goldman has described his parents' personalities as being distinct from their fictional counterparts. Ira, the father in the novel, is warm and doting; he annually excuses his son from school to attend football games at Harvard. In contrast Goldman has explained that his father, who worked as a chemical engineer in a factory that made false teeth, was "pretty violent," adding that, in contrast to how many may think of Jewish men, he was "rough."[1] Their domestic life was chaotic, his parents' relationship was tumultuous, and Goldman has referred to himself as a "survivor" of his home and school.

Within this environment Goldman did not excel academically, although he was drawn to writing, often producing short stories for other students. Some of these stories wound up in the high school literary magazine; meanwhile teachers skeptical of his talent accused him of plagiarism. After high school Goldman attended the private Hobart College in Geneva, New York, but transferred to the University of Michigan, from which he graduated in 1977 with a B.A. After university he moved to New York City, and then, hoping to produce stories to gain entry into M.F.A. programs, he moved to his uncle's house in Guatemala City in 1979, placing himself squarely within one of the most violent periods of that country's history. He explained: "I was in my twenties, and the two parts of the world I am from—the US and Central America—were essentially at war with each other. I wasn't going to miss that."[2] He sold several stories to *Esquire,* and the acquiring editor, Rust Hills, encouraged him to continue his journalistic work, which he did.

In the nearly forty years since he began his career as a journalist and novelist, Goldman has established himself as a unique and important voice in contemporary U.S. literature. His fiction and nonfiction works have earned prizes, and he was named a Guggenheim Fellow in 1998. He has attracted an international readership and has been translated into fifteen languages. He currently splits his time between Mexico City and the United States. At Trinity College in Hartford, Connecticut, he holds the position of Allan K. Smith Professor of English Language and Literature, where he teaches courses in fiction writing and literature.

Goldman's knowledge of Central America and his interest in the region facilitated a significant career as a journalist. He reported on and from Central America in venues with a U.S. audience, allowing U.S. residents to better understand the conflicts that plagued the region during the 1980s and 1990s and the U.S. roles in these conflicts. In a February 1990 report on Nicaragua's national election, Goldman took the United States to task for their newfound and uneven interest in democracy in Central America. "Did men like Reagan and Bush and [assistant secretary of state] Abrams . . . care whether Nicaragua had free and fair elections . . . during the long and brutal rule of General

Anastasio Somoza Debayle?"[3] Goldman's rhetorical question does not necessitate a full response, but he did explain, for those less aware of the recent history of the country, that in fact the United States expressed interest in "free and fair" elections only once the Sandinistas took power in 1979, thereby actually opening up a space for democracy in a nation that, like its Central American neighbors, had heretofore been controlled by an "oligarch-military alliance." Goldman relied on references to U.S. culture and society to translate Nicaraguan events to his readers. Discussing a Sandinista rally he noted that a performer resembled a "*campesino* [farmworker] David Byrne" and remarked that the campaign of incumbent Sandinista president Daniel Ortega had "little to learn from [Fox News executive] Roger Ailes about creating vivid campaign imagery" (74).[4] Goldman's comparison was more apt than he could possibly have predicted as subsequent decades saw both Ortega and Ailes accused of sexual assault, the former by his stepdaughter Zoilamérica and the latter by dozens of women who worked with and for Fox News. The author did suggest that leaders such as Ortega and his vice president, Sergio Ramírez, had a lot to learn and might even benefit from losing the election and being forced to develop their party into a tough opposition force. But Goldman reserved his fiercest critique for U.S. politicians, concluding that it is not for him to decide the fate of Nicaraguan politics, but neither is it the United States' role to do so. Ortega and the Sandinistas, of course, went on to lose the historic election, and the United States did make good on its promise to stop funding the counterrevolutionary army ("Contras"), bringing about a permanent cease-fire to the civil war. However, the fact that Daniel Ortega and a now unrecognizable version of the Sandinista party are in power illustrates that Goldman's articles remain relevant for documenting the long history of U.S. intervention in the country, the opposition to this intervention by U.S. citizens and journalists, and the continued inextricable relation between U.S. and Nicaraguan politics.

While he is well known for his novels—he published three between 1992 and 2004—he has also published book-length works of nonfiction. *The Art of Political Murder: Who Killed the Bishop?*, published in 2007, details Goldman's inquiry into the death of Archbishop Juan Gerardi, who was murdered just days after releasing the Guatemalan Catholic Church's analysis of state-backed violence during that country's thirty-year civil war. In the book, which reads like a political thriller, Goldman detailed Gerardi's last day, interviewed witnesses, walked readers through the possible steps that Gerardi's murderers may have taken to enter his house, and even tracked down exiles who feared for their lives for their part in the trial. The result is a complex portrait of violence and greed that reflects the ongoing war and impunity in Central America. When Goldman pursued a potential witness in Mexico City he did so as a resident of the great metropolis, a city that he has called home for several decades. His more recent work similarly comes from this perspective, as he has often written on Mexican affairs for a U.S. audience. From 2014 to 2015 he wrote a multipart series for the *New Yorker* titled "The Crisis in Mexico," which covered the disappearance of forty-three students from a teacher's school in Iguala, Guerrero. The series explains the relationship between Mexican state and federal authorities (including police and armed forces) and narco-traffickers that has led many Mexican citizens—both residents of large cities and smaller rural towns—to live in a nation beset by corruption and violence. Goldman's insistence on continuing to publish in and for U.S. venues indicates his commitment to not only translating Latin American issues to a U.S. and global audience but also underscoring how interconnected these issues are, particularly for U.S. citizens and residents.

In many ways Goldman's career has been circular; he began as a journalist covering the wars in Central America and now is a frequent contributor to the *New Yorker.* Of his knowledge that one could write both fiction and journalism, he has credited the Colombian master Gabriel García Márquez, who similarly wrote in both genres. In a 1984 piece on the Sandinista popular army published in *Harper's,* Goldman wrote that a political leader's plans for a sugar factory sounded to him like José Buendía's plans to manufacture ice in the jungle, referencing Márquez's *One Hundred Years of Solitude.* The interplay between journalism and fiction links him to a particularly Latin American tradition, as Latin American literary giants including the aforementioned Márquez, as well as Mario Vargas Llosa and Julio Cortazar, also have written journalism and fiction. Rather than viewing these as two separate, discrete branches of writing, however, Goldman has encouraged us to see them as linked: "García Márquez is always saying that journalism—he means narrative journalism—is just another branch of literature, and he's completely right of course."[5] Through his oeuvre we can indeed view both the literary and narrative elements of journalism as well as the influence of journalism on his fiction.

Although Goldman worked throughout the 1980s as a war correspondent in Central America, his interest in and dedication to fiction never wavered. His knowledge of Latin American history, politics, and literature is evident throughout his writings, which incorporate ex-Sandinista soldiers, Guatemalan presidents, and the Cuban independence leader José Martí as characters. All his works traverse the American continents (including the Caribbean) and weave together stories of political intrigue, personal growth, and romantic love. His debut novel, *The Long Night of White Chickens* (1992), grew organically from his early years as a reporter. The work centers on the autobiographical character Rogerio Graetz and Graetz's relationship with his childhood friend and sister-like companion, Flor de Mayo Puac. Flor is also an autobiographical character, modeled on a maid in Goldman's childhood home, who was murdered in Guatemala during a particularly violent period of that country's civil war.[6] The work moves through time and space as Rogerio recalls his and Flor's childhoods in Massachusetts while he pursued her murderer in Guatemala and struggled to come to terms with his friend's decisions and actions after returning to her native country. *The Long Night of White Chickens* received critical acclaim and gathered a committed readership for Goldman.

His second novel, the critically and popularly acclaimed *The Ordinary Seaman,* also reached a wide readership. Published in 1997, the book includes a cast of U.S. and Latin American characters. While deeply rooted in questions of transnational politics and economics, the work also engages with questions of loss, migration, wandering, and love. The story centers on a group of immigrant workers stranded in a Brooklyn harbor because the ship they have been hired to work on, the *Urus,* does not have proper documentation. As the men inhabit a kind of political no man's land, the novel allegorically broaches the contemporary situation of so many undocumented immigrants in the United States today. The text is often read as a meditation on the conditions of labor and living experienced by immigrants to the United States as well as a work that gestures to a postnational world where clearly demarcated borders are blurred.

Following the success of *The Ordinary Seaman,* Goldman took on another ambitious project as he tackled literary and political history in his third novel, *The Divine Husband* (2004). This novel re-creates the time that José Martí, the great Cuban independence fighter and beloved poet, spent in Guatemala. Like Goldman's other texts, *The Divine Husband* weaves together several American stories as it follows Martí from Cuba to Guatemala and the United States, where Martí lived in exile in New York for several years. The novel is astounding for its ability to bring together political and literary history with fiction and romance. While it stems from the story of the affair between Martí and the young Guatemalan woman who inspired Martí's beloved poem "*La niña de Guatemala,*" the novel also writes Martí into the lives of several fictional characters, including the protagonist María de las Nieves Moran.

In his fourth novel, Goldman excavated the tragedy of his own life in a work that hews closely to the story of his marriage to Aura Estrada and of her abrupt death during a holiday in Mexico less than two years after their wedding. Excruciatingly painful and yet artistically beautiful, *Say Her Name* (2011) follows the narrator as he reconstructs the story of their short time together, from their days living in Brooklyn while he wrote and she attended graduate school at Columbia, to their wedding in Mexico and their brief married life.

Following Aura's death Goldman continued to live part time in Mexico City, and the wondrous city is the subject of his most recent work, *The Interior Circuit: A Mexico City Chronicle* (2014). This latest work is in some ways several works in one—it covers Goldman's continuing recovery after his wife's death while the last section recalls *The Art of Political Murder: Who Killed the Bishop?* as well as his journalistic work as Goldman pursues a story about the 2013 kidnapping and murder of thirteen youth outside a nightclub. The case made headlines because it involved a large-scale crime in what was considered a "safe" zone in the city, indicating the extent to which violence and corruption in Mexico continues to cross class and geographic spaces.

Genres

Despite his large and wide-ranging oeuvre, Goldman has engaged consistently with several themes and genres that closely align with major currents of U.S. and Latin American letters. Specifically, we may read him as a writer of historical fiction, as illustrative of transnational literature, as a U.S. Latina/o writer, and as a *crónista* (chronicler). Given its grounding in events such as the Guatemalan civil war and José Marti's life, Goldman's work is undoubtedly historical fiction. He has completed extensive research, but at the same time he has been committed to embellishment and storytelling, and much of his work also has an element of the fantastical. For example, while *The Divine Husband* includes historical characters such as Justo Rufino Barrios (president of Guatemala) and José Martí (Cuban poet and independence leader), the most dynamic characters are the fictional ones—including the protagonist María de las Nieves Moran. The fictional Nieves falls in love with the revered Martí, and their stories in turn intersect with a cast of supporting characters including Jewish Moroccan immigrants to Guatemala (the Nahón family), a Polish businessman (Pryzpyz), and the unlucky-in-love British diplomat (Bludyar). Goldman's work is grounded in history and yet not faithful to it.

In a reflection of his two homes, Goldman has also been committed to drawing equally from U.S. and Latin American sources and references, and his works are dotted with allusions to U.S. and Latin American writers, political leaders, and culture. While it may be tempting to understand his work as engaging in a reconciliation of disparate histories and cultures, it would be more accurate to say that his work excavates the inter-American connections that have long laid beneath U.S.–Latin American (and specifically U.S.–Central American) relations. Thus *The Divine Husband* spends a good deal of time in New York, where Martí spent ten years of his life. In *The Long Night of White Chickens* these connections are more explicitly political—Rogerio recalls his grandmother's support for the CIA-backed coup that toppled Jacobo Árbenz in 1954, and his friend Moya frequently turns to U.S. officials for both information and protection. Likewise, *The Ordinary Seaman* is careful to denote the role that the United States plays in maintaining the state of legal and political limbo that the ship's stateless employees inhabit. In *The Ordinary Seaman* these inter-American connections become increasingly blurry such that the lack of clear national jurisdiction regarding the men's living and working conditions ultimately renders them nationless.

These complex and consistently asserted connections suggest Goldman's work may be classified as "transnational." Within American studies "transnational" as a descriptor of both cultural texts and a critical orientation was asserted most explicitly in the early 2000s; this "transnational turn" in the field "effected the most significant reimagining of the field of American studies since its inception." This transnationalism has allowed scholars to reorient the United States, to place it within a "global economic order," to consider how "the inside and the outside of 'America' . . . are intertwined," and "where more than one location, tradition, or practice comes into play."[7] More specifically, transnational American studies scholarship has considered the Americas more broadly—including the United States, the Caribbean, and Latin America—and in critiquing U.S. exceptionalism has often placed U.S. imperialism in relation to European imperialism. The transnational turn has included the kinds of excavating work that Goldman's fiction performs—highlighting the connections that have always existed between the United States and Latin America. And while Goldman's discussion of incidents such as the CIA overthrow of Árbenz fits in well with the scholarly imperative to examine U.S. imperialism and neocolonialism, his work also portrays transnationalism as a two-way process. That is, his work does not simply suggest that the United States has left indelible marks on places like Guatemala, but that Latin American countries and people have profoundly contributed to the shape of the United States as we know it.

Within the humanities the concept of transnationalism seeks to explain, understand, and ask questions about how individuals and communities define themselves in relation to a nation, or several nations. Michael Templeton has written that "transnational communities undermine the idea that the symbolic structures, political systems, and economic centers singularly define a specific nation." Moreover we need new and different language to describe immigrant experiences, which unfold in a complex, "highly mobile and technologically connected world."[8] Goldman's novels, which always have at least one and usually several binational characters, offer compelling portraits of these kinds of transnational experiences. His language, like that of many contemporary U.S. Latina/o writers, reflects a transnational identity and orientation in its code switching, or use of English and Spanish. While the works are written in English, characters and narrators frequently use a Spanish word or phrase, usually untranslated but intelligible to a monolingual reader through context. The use of Spanish may remind readers that characters are speaking in Spanish while also challenging assumptions about which is the "foreign" language. While Templeton and many critics find the use of Spanish by Latina/o writers a way to reflect "latinization" of the United States, Goldman's relationship to history and historical narratives is also a way of reinserting Spanish into U.S. history. Thus his work reflects increasingly visible Latin American migration to the United States while simultaneously urging us to keep in mind the long history of Spanish-speaking peoples in the United States and long-standing cultural, political, military, and economic ties between the United States and Latin America.

The use of Spanish and storytelling that reflects the perspectives of migrants and immigrants in Goldman's work is common within contemporary U.S. Latina/o literature. Characters such as Rogerio Graetz possess the "double consciousness" that children of immigrants may have—as they live in an in-between space that is neither wholly "American" nor, in Rogerio's case, "Guatemalan."[9] As Goldman once put it, "I feel that I'm *from* Latin America, that I'm as much from *there* as from *here*."[10] Similarly Chicana feminist poet and writer Gloria Anzaldúa drew on her lived experience as a native and resident of the U.S./Mexico border to define the "borderlands" as a state of cultural as well as social and psychological mixture and strength. According to Anzaldúa the competent borderlands inhabitor, *la nueva mestiza* (the new *mestiza*), is characterized by her flexibility, ability to adapt, and "tolerance for ambiguity." An outsider among many cultures she "learns to be an Indian in Mexican culture, to be a Mexican from an Anglo point of view."[11] Like Anzaldúa and other Latinos, Rogerio appears to move relatively easily between U.S. and Guatemalan culture although it is clear that he is also considered an "outsider." He explains that the house he grew up in was known to everyone in his high school as the "Copacabana" because of his mother's kitschy decorations as well as the mere fact that his mother and Flor lived there. And yet Rogerio is also a consummate "American" boy who spends the fall football season accompanying his father to Harvard football games. His ability to move in between languages, cultures, histories, and social strata make him a coresident of Anzaldúa's borderlands.

Goldman's novels include many characters such as Rogerio who move in between U.S. and Latin American cultures frequently; at the same time his works remain invested in representations of marginalized peoples within U.S. and Latin American societies. María from *The Divine Husband* and Flor from *The Long Night of White Chickens* are both indigenous or part-indigenous characters, whose social status is commented on and reinforced by those who occupy a higher social, racial, and economic position than they do. While Goldman's work does not grant extended attention to racialized identity formation, his work's attention to injustice and hierarchies based on race, class, gender, nationality, and citizenship status place the content of his novels firmly in line with themes and perspectives common in U.S. Latina/o literature.

This attention to the intricacies of the human condition may have helped Goldman avoid some of the pitfalls that "ethnic" writers commonly experience. Asked by Whit Coppedge if he was worried about being viewed with a "checklist"—as a "Latino" or "Jewish" writer, Goldman responded that any "checklist problem" has stemmed more from "political correctness and ethnic stereotyping . . . people who think that because there are Central Americans in my book the book must be more about 'being Latino' or 'politics' rather than about all the things the novel is really about, including its manner of telling itself (style, form, genres, etc.)."[12] Goldman went on to divulge that after publishing a book in the United States he has made a habit of inwardly chanting, "Thank god for female reviewers and readers!" because "on the whole it's been women who really seem to get to the emotional heart of my fiction."[13] The author's discussion of the "emotional heart" of his fiction gestures to the deep connections that drive the plot of his novels, even as those works are invariably set during times of intense political upheaval. That "female reviewers and readers" especially connect with his work may also reflect the fact that in the majority of his novels (*The Long Night of White Chickens, The Divine Husband, Say Her Name*), female characters are at the heart of the story's development and narrative.

The reference to a "checklist problem" may be less about trying to pigeonhole a writer or thinker and more about the stark need for a more diverse literary landscape, such that underrepresented and marginalized readers are eager for books and characters that speak to their own often overlooked and ignored histories and experiences. At the same time the fact that Goldman has not run into a "checklist problem" indicates that the constituents to which his books may speak—specifically U.S. Latina/os, Central Americans, and Guatemalan Americans—are not themselves monolithic groups. Thus Goldman is and has been immensely important to the sizable group of people in the United States who identify as Central American and to the growing field of Central American–American studies. That these communities can embrace Goldman without his work being *only* identified with them speaks both to the diversity within Central American communities and Goldman's own skill and breadth as a writer. Moreover, rather than indicate that Goldman has avoided a "problem," the breadth of the constituencies by which he is embraced and his success can also be attributed to the deep-seated connections between the nation-states, cultures, and literary traditions within which he is situated. He is not exclusively a "Latino writer" because he writes about Guatemala; he is an "American" writer because U.S. Latina/os, Guatemalans, and Mexicans have always been and are today "American."

While Goldman is most definitely an "American" writer—in the broad, hemispheric, multilingual sense of the term—he is clearly tied most closely to two countries in the Americas—the United States and Guatemala. His rendering of José Marti in *The Divine Husband,* for example, does not center on Cuba. Rather the text writes Martí into Guatemalan and U.S. history, simultaneously arguing for the transnational circuit of his life and work while specifying the importance of those two locations. These links place Goldman within a U.S. Latina/o and specifically a Central American and Central American–American literary field. As Guatemalan American critic and novelist Arturo Arias has written, the term Central American–American is a "linguistic oddity" and a "dissonance" that "underlines the fact that it is an identity which is not one, since it cannot be designated univocally either as 'Latino' or 'Latin American,' but is outside those two signifiers from the very start."[14] The "diasporic consciousness" that pervades much of Goldman's writing allows his work to both reflect and inaugurate a specifically Central American–American literature and experience (185).

While the content of his work embraces U.S.- and Latin American–based themes and events, the form of his writing similarly draws from several traditions. His long-form, narrative journalism is exemplary of *crónica*. Jennifer Harford Vargas and Monica Hanna have explained that the *crónica,* or chronicle, is a well-known and well-studied genre within Latin American studies that has not received complementary recognition within American studies. The tradition is most closely related with advocacy journalism in the United States and eschews the "objectivity" of conventional journalism by placing the writer within the story, as the author asserts his or her subjectivity and relation to the material at hand. The tradition may be linked to the Conquest of the Americas, when Spanish conquerors offered accounts of their experiences in the New World, but its contemporary form is most closely linked to writers of the late nineteenth and early twentieth centuries, including the Cuban José Martí and Nicaraguan Rubén Darío. Contemporary chroniclers from Latin America and the United States include the Mexicans Elena Poniatowska and Carlos Monsiváis and the U.S. Latina/os Sonia Nazario, Daniel Alarcón, Hector Tobar, and Goldman himself. Within the United States these writers often cover issues of immigration, particularly the plight of undocumented migrants and the dangerous journeys many take through Central America and Mexico to arrive.

Goldman's work focuses less on immigration and more on the legacies of war, violence, political corruption, and U.S. intervention in Guatemala and Mexico. Moreover, he has written of his personal connections to the places and people he has covered. In *The Art of Political Murder: Who Killed the Bishop?* he never shied away from including his own relationship with Guatemalan politics. Similarly, in *The Interior Circuit,* whose subtitle ("A Mexico City Chronicle") overtly evokes the tradition, Goldman often referenced his knowledge of people and places in Mexico, some gained through his late wife, Aura. In addition, he has evinced a keen understanding of audience for his U.S.-based work. Writing about the ongoing search for justice for forty-three students disappeared from Iguala, Guerrero, Mexico, in September 2014, Goldman occasionally has mentioned the political and social atmosphere in his adopted hometown of Mexico City, but his pieces largely conform to accepted U.S. norms and speak in a more detached, neutral tone.

What is also unique and yet often overlooked is the humor that permeates Goldman's work. This aspect of his work is important to Goldman, who remarked in an interview: "I am absolutely baffled when I run into a reader or reviewer who fails to see the humor in my writing . . . or understand how important the role of humor and irony is. Humor is one of my crucial tools."[15] His narrators and protagonists often deploy sardonic, dark, or ironic humor that matches the mostly somber subject matter of his books. In *The Long Night of White Chickens,* Rogerio relates that when he was working as a bartender in New York, he was only ever able to come up with two jokes when one was requested by a patron; both of them center on Chupina (Germán Chupina Barahona), the head of the Guatemalan National Police, who was well known for his role in extensive human rights abuses during his time in power (1978–82). Rogerio recalls: "One joke going around was, Did you hear Chupina had a twin brother in the womb? Yes, stillborn, showing signs of torture and a *tiro de gracias,* a coup de grace, in the head. And in another Chupina and [then president] General Lucas are fishing, and Lucas catches a tiny fish and he's about to toss it back but Chupina says, Wait, give it to me, and he takes the fish in one hand and starts pummeling its head with the other saying, Ok, talk, where are the big ones?"[16] The jokes are funny, bleakly so, and are based on knowledge about the violence and corruption in Guatemala as well as the necessity of laughter as an outlet from the seemingly inescapable darkness.

In addition, Goldman's humor often occurs alongside circular or repetitive elements of his writing so that readers are able to "get" a joke based on having read an earlier section of a book. For example, much of *The Interior Circuit* is devoted to Goldman learning to drive in Mexico City. To get to know the city, he randomly chose a neighborhood from the massive city street guide—*La*

Guia Roji—and attempted to find it. Along the way he translated and explained the sometimes peculiar names of streets and neighborhoods. When he came across a street with the Nahuatl name "Tonacatecuatl," he turned to an expert, who informed him that the name may come from the word "Tonakatekwani," meaning "our meat of the jaguar" (135). Goldman admitted that the translation remains opaque—does this mean "'this jaguar meat that we're going to eat' or 'jaguar meat that is corporeally or spiritually a part of who we are'? I don't know" (135). He eventually arrived at the street and attempted to talk to an elderly man selling chickens outside of a small store. When the man indicated his lack of interest in talking with him, the writer explained: "He was in no mood to talk, this old Aztec merchant with his festering clumps of jaguar meat" (143–44). The reference to jaguar meat then becomes a sort of inside joke between the writer and his readers, and "getting" the joke functions as a reward for having read earlier portions of the text and for remaining at Goldman's side through the literary adventure of his narrative.

Finally, while Goldman is of Jewish descent, he has engaged with themes of Judaism and Jewish American-ness only obliquely in his work, such that it is difficult to accurately describe him as a Jewish American or Jewish Latina/o writer. Nevertheless, Jewish characters are found in almost all his novels, albeit often in passing. Despite this lack of explicit engagement with themes or topics we may deem "Jewish," Goldman's work is marked by this heritage, and his father's lineage is often remarked on and described in biographical work and interviews. His Jewish-ness is easily recognizable as he possesses, in the words of the narrator of *Say Her Name,* "the planet's most Jewish-sounding surname" (193). In a U.S. culture that is still overly reliant on a black/white view of race and ignorant of multiracial, multinational identities, Goldman's ethnicity is often misunderstood. In an autobiographical essay, "Moro Like Me," he related the absurd moment in which a childhood acquaintance disputed his identity, going so far as to fax a local newspaper to do so. During an interview with a paper located near the small town where he grew up, the interviewer reported that they had received "a rather disturbing fax" from someone who had "taken offense" to Goldman's self-identity as Guatemalan American (62). The childhood acquaintance seemed to think that this "Jewish kid" could not possibly *also* be Guatemalan American. Stating the obvious the writer responded: "Well, Goldman. Hello? My last name *is* Goldman," and he then explained to the interviewer how ridiculous it would have been for him to have gone "marching through the halls of [his] high school asserting [his] 'Guatemalan roots'" (62, 63). He also questioned for whose benefit such kinds of ethnic articulations would be when he asserted he would not "spend [his] writing career justifying to Americans how you can be half Jewish and *latinoamericano,* too" (64). The essay effectively portrayed Goldman's binationality as well as the instability and relativity of racial recognition. In the mostly Irish Italian town where he grew up, the author's Jewish-ness was the most salient marker of difference. But in other contexts, such as when he has been repeatedly stopped by police in Spain who suspect him of having *moro*—North African—heritage, his difference has been marked by his dark skin, hair, and eyes. These incidents illustrate the futility of trying to apply static, monolithic notions of race in a world that is, and always has been, much more complex.

CHAPTER 2

Searching for Self and Confronting Impunity in *The Long Night of White Chickens*

Goldman's debut novel, *The Long Night of White Chickens* (1992), grew directly out of his experiences writing about the Guatemalan civil war as well as his own background as Guatemalan American. The text earned critical and popular acclaim. Wallace Shawn of the *Village Voice* declared the novel was "hardly a standard fictional debut,"[1] while Constance Casey of the *New York Times* named the work "a solidly realistic and richly detailed evocation of what it's like to live in Guatemala."[2] The book's engagement with a wide expanse of material—ranging from the Guatemalan civil war and its aftermath to the bicultural experiences of its narrator—is noteworthy but also led some to criticize its potential overreach. As Arturo Arias noted, Goldman's interest in exploring the inner psychological worlds of his characters comes at the cost of a plot that moves little. The structure of the story, which takes the form of a "meandering, late-night conversation,"[3] is also at times "repetitive"[4] and caused one reviewer to designate the narrator, Rogerio Graetz, "incompetent."[5] Still the novel was, and remains, one of the few published in English to address Guatemalan-U.S. history, relations, and identities, and it earned several well-deserved prizes, including the Sue Kaufman Prize for First Fiction and a designation as a finalist for the P.E.N./Faulkner Award. Four important elements mark the text: the representation of binationality on the part of the protagonist and his own psychic journey; the engagement with Guatemalan history and U.S. intervention in the region; the collusion between military, government, and media actors in contributing to an ongoing state of impunity; and Goldman's characteristic use of dark humor in the weaving of a tale that is intelligently self-referencing.

The Long Night of White Chickens centers on Rogerio Graetz—the son of a poor Boston Jew and a wealthy Guatemalan *mestiza*. Early in his childhood, his mother, determined to leave her husband, returns to her native Guatemala with her young son. However, once Rogerio contracts tuberculosis, she returns to her husband to raise him in suburban Boston. Rogerio, who narrates the majority of novel, explains that "we went back to Massachusetts for the better hospitals in Boston, and also because Abuelita [Grandma] had my mother convinced that my illness was punishment from God for having abandoned my father up there" (3). Rogerio's early years are ones of isolation; his illness compounded with the cultural otherness between himself and his peers means that he passes many hours watching the lives of his neighbors unfold from afar. Abuelita, Rogerio's Guatemalan grandmother, offers her middle-class version of long-distance care by "sending" the Graetz family a *muchacha* to help care for Rogerio and perform housework in the Graetz home. An orphan from the department of Chiquimula, Flor de Mayo Puac becomes an integral part of the Graetz family: she functions as a sister to Rogerio and a daughter to Mr. Graetz. Flor's status within the family, which involves a trespassing of lines of race and class according to Guatemalan society, becomes a source of stress for Mirabel, Rogerio's mother. This stress turns to shame twenty years later when Flor is found murdered, her death tied to her own criminal activities.

Flor's tragic death stands in contrast to her time with the Graetz family in Massachusetts, where she grows up alongside Rogerio. As he explains: "because [his father] was never comfortable with the idea of having a maid in the first place, and did not think a thirteen-year-old girl should spend all day housecleaning in a house where there wasn't all that much to clean, my father decided that Flor should go to school" (4). As she speaks no English, Flor is initially enrolled in first grade with Rogerio, but she advances quickly, graduating from high school several years before him and going on to attend Wellesley College. Despite, or perhaps because of, her success in the United States, Flor returns to Guatemala City in the late 1970s, where she becomes the director of a private orphanage and malnutrition clinic, Los Quetzalitos.[6] A few years after returning, when she is in her early thirties, Flor is found mysteriously murdered, stabbed in the throat in her bedroom in the orphanage. Newspapers in Guatemala City speculate that Flor's death was a result of her using Los Quetzalitos as a means to process illegal adoptions and that her death came at the hands of one of her criminal associates. When the narrative opens, Flor has been found dead, and Rogerio and his father, Ira, have flown to Guatemala City to bring her body back to the States. The subsequent narrative is composed of decades of Rogerio's memories, stemming from his childhood with Flor through visits he took to Guatemala to see her when both were adults. These memories are interspersed with his own present-day travels to Guatemala and inquiries into Flor's death. Much of the novel is an attempt at reconciliation, as Rogerio tries to understand the relationship between the children and adults that he and Flor were and became. Rogerio's explorations are personal and political, geographic and psychological, and he is joined throughout most of them by his childhood friend Luis Moya Martínez, a Guatemalan newspaper reporter.[7] Through Rogerio, Moya (the name he is called by all characters in the novel), and their investigations, *The Long Night of White Chickens* tells a story that is at once sentimental and tragic and sheds light on the complicated relationships between the United States and Guatemala in the aftermath of the Guatemalan civil war and amid ongoing violence and impunity in Central America.

Binationality and Psychological Explorations

Rogerio's trip to claim Flor's body and search for her murderer reflects his need to reconcile his binational self and his relationship with the murdered young woman. The trip to recover Flor's body lasts only a few days, but when he returns to Guatemala to continue his investigation several years later, readers understand that this quest remains an ongoing, unfinished process. Of course Rogerio is not the only character to return to Guatemala in search of his origins, Flor herself engaged in the same reverse migration when she moved back to Guatemala City after college. According to Linda J. Craft, all three of the novel's main characters—Rogerio, Flor, and Moya—are engaged in a search for their origins. The critic explained that although the novel is structured as a search for Flor's murderer(s), it is really a search for self; nevertheless "the novel announces quite early and repeatedly the impossibility of determining origins and destinies."[8] The impossibility of determining origins is explicable in Flor's case; she herself is an orphan with limited knowledge about her family and background but is also portrayed as the result of geographic and psychic knots that cannot be fully unraveled. Thus the novel suggests that there is no singular origin; at the very least, characters such as Rogerio and Flor are equally rooted in two nations and places. These multiple roots and trajectories are reflected in the novel's structure and style, which relies largely on Rogerio to narrate but consistently weaves in other characters' thoughts, perspectives, and memories. Some may view these narrative choices as a reflection of Rogerio's "incompetence"[9] as a narrator or his "confusion"[10] concerning his identity. However, the work suggests that it is the nature of humans, or at least the humans in this work, to remain searching, regardless of whatever information they may find. After all, very early in the text Rogerio tells readers that while he and his father were in Guatemala to recover Flor's body and inquire about the circumstances of her death, "nothing happened to convince us that what the papers and authorities were saying about Flor wasn't true. Nothing."[11] And yet the narrative, and Rogerio's dual search for self and for Flor, continue for an additional 450 pages. Thus we are presented with a journey of self-exploration that is potentially both limitless and futile.

The psychic journey that the novel focuses on is an appropriate, but underutilized, mode of writing about conflict and trauma. Guatemalan-born critic and writer Arturo Arias explained that the novel's ability to offer to English-speaking, North American readers a glimpse of the interior lives of its characters is one of the work's principal accomplishments. Arias suggested that the trauma of the thirty-six-year-long civil war has caused Guatemalans to stifle their emotions such that many Guatemalan novels that deal with the conflict are more descriptive. Goldman, on the other hand, is "Guatemalan enough" to connect to feelings shared widely by Guatemalans while also "American enough" to marvel at Guatemalan reticence to verbalize anxiety. As a result, the novel portends future literary works that represent bicultural and global identities and experiences.[12]

As Arias noted, Goldman harnesses his own life in the service of creating his emotionally complex characters; autobiographical elements of the novel include Rogerio's own racial and cultural background, his ties to Guatemala and Flor, and some of his experiences in Guatemala. In addition to the shared heritage between Goldman and Rogerio, Flor is an amalgamation of several maids that the Goldman family had during his childhood in Needham, Massachusetts, one of whom was murdered and whose death Goldman and a friend investigated.[13] The inclusion of Moya as a central character reflects both Goldman's own experiences as a journalist and his friendship with Guatemalan journalists of the time period. Goldman worked as a journalist during the 1980s, writing about the conflicts in Central America for magazines such as *Esquire* and *Harper's*. He has explained that journalism also functions as a metaphor for the wars in Central America, in which wars were not "just over bodies and bullets but over words, over which description of the events and the reasons for those events would carry the day."[14]

His deep knowledge of the country and interest in journalism granted him a unique perspective on the relationship between the civil war and its impact on the press. In a piece published in *Harper's* several years prior to the publication of *The Long Night of White Chickens*, the author lamented the sad state of freedom of the press in Central America. Addressing Guatemalan periodicals directly he noted that in a nation where the average worker brings home $35 per month, the back pages of the leading daily paper, *Prensa Libre*, are nevertheless filled with advertisements for luxury items and expensive cars.[15] This disconnect between the lives of common citizens and what appears in newspapers is addressed in a darkly comedic episode in *The Long Night of White Chickens.* After a hippopotamus from the national zoo dies, its carcass is taken to the city dump, and the next day two newspapers report that the people who scavenge the dump for sustenance have started to eat the hippopotamus meat. But of course, Moya relates to Rogerio, "newspapers reach the garbage dump on the same day they are published, and at least a few of its resident scavengers were able to read" (263). The example portrays the lack of knowledge regarding the lives of the poorest Guatemalans on the part of national elites and the media that serve them.

The nonchronological structure of the novel emphasizes the deep-rooted connections between Rogerio's two countries. The work constantly crisscrosses between the two settings and primarily among the cities of Boston, New York, and Guatemala City. For example, the first two pages of the novel cover over twenty years of Rogerio's life, including his move to Guatemala as a child, his return to Boston, Flor's arrival, and his and Ira's trip to recover Flor's body. The narrative remains neither in Guatemala nor the past, coming instead to rest in the near present, "the day just over a month ago," when Rogerio received a phone call from his childhood friend Moya. Within the first five pages then, the novel has moved from Boston to Guatemala and back again and introduced the text's principal characters—Rogerio, his parents, Flor, and Moya—presenting a complicated entryway to a story that nevertheless remains focused on these five individuals as their lives move between two nations and roughly three decades of history.

While the novel offers up the opportunity for Goldman to represent and reflect on his own childhood and ties to Guatemala, the narrative is also an opportunity for the protagonist to engage in a transnational process of self-exploration. The deep psychological ties between Rogerio and Flor mean that his investigation into her death cannot be anything less than an investigation into his own psyche and affective ties with the country of his mother's birth as well as his relationship with Flor and his childhood. Of course what connects Rogerio to Guatemala are two women—his mother, Mirabel Arrau, and Flor—meaning that his exploration is deeply gendered. Throughout the text Mirabel Arrau is represented as someone who Rogerio knows well; he is able to characterize her as an at times rigid, but deeply loving woman and mother. The portrait of Flor is decidedly more complicated as the novel largely centers on Rogerio's explorations into whether the woman he thought he knew so well could have been involved with people and crimes seemingly so outside her values and personality. One aspect of Flor's life with which Rogerio is confronted is her sexuality; as he looks for her murderers he attempts to understand her romantic affairs. While Rogerio narrates this aspect of his investigation he does not express any discomfort, but as his investigations continue he involves himself in a bizarre and dangerous sexual relationship, suggesting the extent to which his explorations have taken a toll on his own mental and emotional health.

Rogerio's investigations into Flor's death necessitate searching for her connections to powerful men and lead Rogerio and Moya to learn of her affair with Celso Batres, an important social and political figure.[16] Batres is the owner of several newspapers in Guatemala, including the daily *El Minuto* for which Moya writes (178). Rogerio and Moya spend some time puzzling over the identity of a secret married lover, whom Flor had mentioned to Rogerio in their last conversation before her death. Later Rogerio reveals to Moya that an employee of the orphanage that Flor ran confirmed that her lover was indeed Batres. In a manner typical of the circular, self-referencing narrative, readers learn of Batres's relationship with Flor as an aside in a conversation between Rogerio and Moya but then are given more details and transported into a more distant past, through Rogerio's conversations with Flor's employee. The effect is that readers have the sense of piecing together the details of Flor's life, first receiving small bits of information before a more complete picture is revealed.

Rogerio also reveals that Moya and Flor were lovers, albeit briefly. As their investigations and conversations continue, the two realize that Flor in fact dated Moya while on a brief hiatus from her relationship with Batres. She apparently returned to Batres a month before her death. While Moya claims he dated Flor only "un poquito" [a little], their relationship is significant to both him as a person and the overall novel (270). The title of the novel is taken from a date between Moya and Flor at a Chinese restaurant in Zone 9 of Guatemala City, Fo Lu Shu II. The two characters spend hours eating dinner and drinking rum, remaining so late as to witness workers at the restaurant bringing in live chickens to prepare for the next day. The hauling in of chickens becomes a metaphor for Guatemala. Flor complains: "I'm sure Frank Perdue doesn't carry all his chickens to his slaughterhouse one by one. But everything gets done here in some stupid, slow, and inevitably cruel way, doesn't it?" (314). Flor's reference of the U.S. agro-business giant Perdue speaks to her own American-ness, but her indictment of Guatemala comes from a place of deep knowledge and affection. For his part Moya is so entranced by Flor and what they witness at the restaurant that he "forever referred to [that night] as the Long Night of White Chickens" (315). This mix of morbidity and fantasy, the use of a fairy-tale-like title to name a scene that included the death of dozens of fowl, is characteristic of the novel and the principal characters' use of humor and irony in the face of death and destruction.

The discoveries of Flor's relationship with Moya and Batres are somewhat paralleled in Rogerio's own life as toward the end of the narrative he becomes involved with a Guatemalan woman who is herself also involved with a powerful public figure. Claiming that frequenting low-class brothels will be a good way to come in contact with people involved in the baby trade and thus will perhaps yield further clues to Flor's life and death, Rogerio develops a relationship with a sex worker, Zamara. He begins to visit her frequently, drinking throughout her shift as a dancer. Zamara, however, is involved with a lieutenant in the Guatemalan Army, and Rogerio's interest in her places them both at risk. Here we can see a parallel between the triangular relationships among Batres, Flor, and Moya. In this new incarnation, Batres is replaced by Lieutenant Nub, Flor by Zamara, and Moya of course by Rogerio. In this reworked love triangle, the novel hints at Rogerio's complicated relationship to Flor as well as his deep connection to Moya. These elements of the novel also underscore the significant psychological journey that Rogerio undertakes in his search for Flor's murderer.

Some experiences detailed in the novel draw from Goldman's own life. Toward the end of the novel, after becoming involved with Zamara, Rogerio worries about his safety. He sets up a home-alarm system in his grandmother's house, which consists of strategically placed glass bottles and a rope to escape. In his 2007 nonfiction account of the murder of Bishop Juan Gerardi, Goldman talked about this time period in his own life, which occurred when he lived in the country from 1984 to 1985. He wrote: "I rigged up homemade alarms in my grandmother's house: glass bottles on chairs beneath every window, an escape rope leading onto the patio."[17] Goldman's recollections illustrate the palpable danger that even U.S. citizens living in Guatemala faced during the civil war and suggest Rogerio's preoccupations are well founded.

Of course Guatemalans without access to the protections of U.S. citizens, including members of Goldman's family, faced extensive danger. In a small aside in *The Long Night of White Chickens,* Rogerio mentions his uncle, Dr. Nelson Arrau. He explains that the doctor had sought to start a rural health program, training "barefoot doctors" in the countryside. But the regime considered training students, who Rogerio refers to as "rural Johnny Appleseeds" distributing dysentery pills, to be "completely Communistic," and Dr. Arrau was forced into exile.[18] In his later nonfiction work Goldman explained that his uncle was politically conservative and a deeply religious Catholic who was committed to public health. But he fled the country once several of the rural doctors he trained were murdered and a small public clinic he'd built was confiscated by the army. (Goldman, Art of Political Murder, 16) Goldman's uncle, and his fictional representative, Dr. Arrau, inspired a similar figure in John

Sayles's 1997 movie *Men with Guns.* Sayles's film, set in an unnamed Latin American country, follows Dr. Fuentes, who seeks to find answers regarding the murders of his former students, confronting guerrillas and soldiers in the remote countryside as he does so. Sayles credited Goldman and other friends in the production notes for the film.[19] In a piece posted on the film's website Goldman confirmed the connection between his uncle and Dr. Fuentes but clarified that unlike the unsuspecting physician in the movie, his uncle was never "innocent about the violence in the countryside" even though he did not think that the army would go so far as to murder rural doctors.[20] The trauma as a result of the murders did cause his uncle to suffer a major, paralyzing stroke, and the same thing happens to Rogerio's uncle in *The Long Night of White Chickens*.[21]

The novel also draws from Goldman's life when it describes how Moya and Rogerio narrowly escape an attempted kidnapping. Rogerio tells how, en route to a store, the two notice a black Jeep Cherokee, slowly driving along the street across from them, slowing when they stop walking and continuing when they continue. At this point in the novel, Rogerio has referenced the ominous Jeep Cherokees, which were notorious for their use by death squads, several times so that readers also understand their significance. Rogerio narrates: "I touched Moya and we looked at it and froze, but the Jeep came to a stop too, and we thought, No, it can't be, and started walking again . . . it was just like [what I] always . . . imagined . . . it would be like to see a shark circling and then there it was, circling. Instead of running, we stopped again. Now all four doors opened. They came out, three of them carrying Uzis, machine guns" (384). In a split-second reaction Rogerio pulls Moya down behind an ambulance parked on the street, and just then a city bus comes down the street, and the two men "[run] along with the bus like a shield between [them] and [jump] onto it while it [is] still accelerating down the street!" (384). In his later works *The Art of Political Murder* and *The Interior Circuit,* published in 2007 and 2014 respectively, Goldman revisited the experience behind this event: "There was that late afternoon in Guatemala City in 1984 when Jean-Marie Simon, the photographer and human rights reporter, and I were walking from the apartment we shared . . . to the corner store when four men got out of a black Cherokee that had been tailing us and drew weapons out through the open doors, but we 'escaped' by throwing ourselves down behind the row of parked ambulances in front of a small private hospital, and then we got up and sprinted alongside a bus that suddenly drove between them and us and jumped onto it, and the Cherokee rocketed away down the long straight avenue, running red lights."[22] In the novel version of the events, Rogerio is describing the incident to his lover at the time and adds that the two men rode the bus to the outer edge of the city, shaking and trying to calm down. But Goldman's nonfiction account contains even more incredible details as he explained that after going to the U.S. embassy to report the incident, which the U.S. consul somehow already knew about, he was told that the kidnappers could have murdered him if they had wanted but that instead, the incident was "a heavy-handed tail, meant to send a message."[23] Goldman explained that despite the warning neither he nor Simon left the country. "I didn't have the money for a plane ticket, and at that time I had no real place to go home to. Jean-Marie simply had too much important work in Guatemala, and wasn't going to leave."[24] Years later, Goldman ran into the U.S. diplomat in Mexico City where the diplomat said he could not believe the two had not left the country.

Goldman's use of own experiences, which were unique for Guatemala at that time only insofar as he escaped unharmed, blurs the line between fiction and nonfiction. As the author affirmed in his assessment of *Men with Guns,* the violence depicted is not only "believable" but also happened.[25] The overlap between Goldman's life and that of his characters speaks to the importance of literature in reflecting that which may be unimaginable, but is nevertheless necessary to confront. By way of offering some hope in the face of this reality, Goldman reported that the clinic that his uncle started is thriving and has trained thousands of health technicians in the last decades. He concluded that "the possibility for peace remains, even in a country as troubled as Guatemala."[26]

U.S. Intervention

Rogerio's binational upbringing represents that of Goldman's as well as the long-standing history of U.S. involvement in the region. The year 1954 is often used to mark a turning point in both U.S. intervention and modern Guatemalan history; that year a CIA-backed coup helped to overthrow the democratically elected government of Jacobo Árbenz. In his later work *The Art of Political Murder,* Goldman offered a concise explanation for U.S. attention to the country, which largely stemmed from economic interests in the form of the United Fruit Company. The UFC held considerable sway within the administration of President Dwight Eisenhower, through his secretary of state, John Foster Dulles, and CIA director Allen Dulles. Prior to taking office, Foster Dulles had worked in a New York law firm that helped the UFC negotiate a very favorable transportation deal in Guatemala, which allowed the banana company to transport their product from plantations to coastal areas cheaply and efficiently. Árbenz threatened UFC power and profits when he signed an agrarian reform law that would redistribute privately owned, fallow land to landless peasants. As the single biggest landowner in the country, UFC had much to lose from this reform. Árbenz's opponents, including the Dulles brothers, leveraged charges of communism against him, a serious indictment during this time period of the Cold War. In fact, Árbenz had legalized the small Guatemalan communist party, and members of the party were represented in his cabinet, although they were small in number and not very powerful. The land reform law did not eschew compensation to private interests but in a stroke of genius (or perhaps political suicide) included the provision that companies would be reimbursed according to the stated value of the land on their taxes. Of course the UFC had underreported the value of their land and thus were left with the possibility of being compensated for their own proclaimed, lower value.[27] These subtleties, as well as the right of foreign peoples to elect their own leaders, were lost on the Dulles brothers, who used their influence to engineer the 1954 coup. They initiated the first (but certainly not the last) CIA coup of a democratically elected foreign leader in Latin America. After ousting Árbenz (who sought asylum in Mexico and committed suicide years later), the United States handed over power to wealthy landowners and political elites, who maintained power through paramilitary forces and the Guatemalan Army. This army, which continued to receive aid from the United States, would become, in Goldman's words "the most brutal, corrupt, and criminal military institution in the western hemisphere."[28] These events mark the start of the Guatemalan civil war, which would continue until the signing of peace accords in 1996.

In *The Long Night of White Chickens* Rogerio references the CIA-backed coup that ousted Árbenz several times in the narrative. Midway through the novel he recalls how he educated himself on Guatemala by reading a wide range of social, political, and historical books. Explaining the Leftist orientation of many of these works he says: "Four hundred years of repressing the Indian majority, dictatorship after dictatorship, one decade of democracy ended by a U.S.-sponsored coup that issued in the current thirty years of military rule—understandably, the Rightist Latinist is likely to find more that interests him in, say, Cuba" (184). His indictment of both Guatemalan racism and classism and U.S. intervention continues, and he does not shy away from speaking of the complicity of his own Guatemalan family. He explains that Abuelita had helped to overthrow Árbenz by "defying the government-imposed blackout of the capital by lighting charcoal in a pit in her patio and fanning it while she stared up at the sky" (201). Abuelita was cheering the country's liberation from "Communism" although Rogerio says that she was unaware of the CIA's role in the coup, "not that she would have regretted it much, or at all" (201).

The text necessarily references this history; however most of the novel takes place later in the twentieth century, during the bloodiest years of the civil war, when the country was ruled by General Romeo Lucas García and government-backed violence was rampant. Because many of Rogerio's friends and associates are wealthy residents of the capital, they are also subject to violence from guerrillas, who Rogerio explains were responsible for the attempted kidnapping and death of one of his cousin's classmates. However, he also places some blame on the young man himself for refusing to be kidnapped because, as Rogerio explains, "he could have had a chance to live. His family could have paid the ransom" (18). This option is not afforded to those who were kidnapped by the police and military; he continues: "Of course the people who the army and the police took or killed were rarely given the option of paying ransom. And they took or killed thousands upon thousands" (19). Here Rogerio references the disparate deaths that came at the hands of guerrillas as opposed to those that came at the hands of police, military, and paramilitary forces. Several years after the peace accords were signed in 1996, the Human Rights Office of the Archdiocese of the Catholic Church released an extensive report on the violence, published in English as *Guatemala: Never Again!* The report, known also by its Spanish acronym REMHI (Recuperación de la Memoria Histórica), consists of testimony covering the thirty-six-year-long civil war. Rogerio's account of the atrocities is in line with that of the REMHI report, which found that the majority of human rights violations occurred between 1980 and 1983 (Flor is killed on February 17, 1983) and attributes most of these abuses to the U.S.-backed Guatemalan military. Estimates indicate that over two hundred thousand people were killed and millions displaced. Recent scholarship has traced the continuing violence in the region from the 1954 coup through the civil war period and into the postconflict period, emphasizing the ongoing state of impunity that exists.

Read within this context, the lack of an indicted criminal for Flor's murder represents the lack of accountability for thousands of Guatemalan deaths. In his review in the *Los Angeles Times* Guatemalan-born writer Victor Perera wrote: "Flor's murderer will never be known, any more than we will ever discover the authors responsible for the 40,000 'disappeared' and unaccounted for over the past thirty years, not to mention the 100,000 or so Guatemalans known to have been assassinated by the military."[29] This metaphor, in which we may understand Flor's corpse to stand in for the thousands of murdered and disappeared Guatemalans, allows the country itself "to occupy the emotional centre of the novel."[30] As a reporter who wrote about conflicts in Central America throughout the 1970s and 1980s and as a Guatemalan American, Goldman was well positioned to write a novel that takes place during the civil war. Moreover, as a character, Rogerio's binational heritage as well as level of education concerning the United States and Guatemala allow him to understand and comment on the history and continued impact of U.S.-backed conflict in his mother's homeland.

The repression of indigenous communities—again a result of both racism and classism on the part of Guatemala's *mestizo* population as well as a U.S.-backed anticommunist imperative—is likewise mentioned throughout the novel. When they are both adults, Flor tells Rogerio about the Guatemalan Army's establishment of "model villages," communities founded supposedly to keep refugees safe but designed to disrupt and control indigenous life. Rogerio calls these villages a "masterstroke" of the army as they "shatter and reorganize the hermetic pattern of four hundred years of post-Conquest highland life, bringing it all under military control." (Goldman, Long Night of White Chickens, 79) Documents declassified in the 1990s indicate that the United States was well aware of the Guatemalan Army's "scorched earth" policies in the highlands and that the Reagan administration understood its support for Guatemala to be part of a larger anticommunist strategy.

U.S. support for genocidal campaigns in the Guatemalan highlands is largely discussed obliquely by characters in the novel, but this history also lays the groundwork for one of the text's major plot points, Flor's alleged illegal adoption business. The instability and bloodshed disproportionally impacted indigenous communities and resulted in thousands of displaced children and orphans. Rogerio explains that the rule of General Ríos Montt in the early 1980s "added tens of thousands of new orphans to Guatemala's already huge orphan population" (4).[31] Some of these orphans end up in Flor's orphanage, Los Quetzalitos, and she discusses with Rogerio the impact of the war on the children and institution. For example, without proper paperwork certifying that a child is an orphan, the child cannot be adopted, and the children often react in terror to the sight of military trucks. Of course, according to those who believe the accusations against Flor, she did indeed arrange for children to be adopted by foreigners without the proper paperwork. Thus, through Flor's status as the director of an orphanage, the novel engages consistently with some of the aftereffects of U.S. intervention in Guatemala.

According to Victor Perera, the violence is the drug at the heart of the novel, such that it pervades the text and overshadows characters to become the protagonist.[32] Perera conceded however, that Flor's story is significant and that she and her tragic life provide an apt metaphor for the story of Guatemala, a country, like its people, rife with contradictions and contingencies. The violence of which Perera spoke has multiple sources and is implicated through media, government, and military, making Flor's story, and particularly the crime that allegedly leads to her murder, a perfect microcosm for examining Guatemala during and just after the civil war.

Similarly, the crime of which Flor is accused, "selling" children orphaned by the civil war, illuminates the confusing social situation and the genocidal policies carried out against the Mayan population during the war. *Guatemala: Never Again!* details how Mayan peoples and cultural practices were targeted by the government army, leading to widespread familial and ethnic destruction and an ongoing legacy of impunity and lack of safety. Flor's status as the director of an adoption agency puts her in touch with Mayan orphans, allowing the novel to discuss the genocide against the indigenous Guatemalan population. Marc Zimmermann agreed that the subject of adoption is an excellent way to approach civil war and post–civil war Guatemalan society, noting that "no other theme [than that of the supposed selling of Guatemalan babies for organ transplants] can better encompass this period of intense war in the highlands or the continuing efforts to find a base for social peace in the 1990s."[33] Zimmerman's reference to "the highlands" points out how the text broaches violence against indigenous peoples, the majority of whom are located in the highland regions. *Guatemala: Never Again!* also discusses "cases of children who were separated from their families or communities, abducted, and fraudulently adopted by the perpetrators of violence against their families."[34] This legacy of violence and trauma continues to plague Guatemalan communities, particularly indigenous ones. Throughout the 1990s and into the year 2000, several incidents of violence against tourists were perpetuated by local populations who suspected foreigners of trying to steal babies. These include the 1994 beating of a U.S. journalist, the 1997 beating of a Guatemalan woman, and the 2000 murder of a Japanese tourist and Guatemalan bus driver.[35]

The discussion of the adoption scheme and how it is handled by the Guatemalan government and press also allows the text to bring to light deep-seated resentment and skepticism on the part of Guatemalans toward the United States. Speaking with Consul Simms in Guatemala City, Rogerio and his father are told that there are rumors that not only Flor, but anyone doing U.S. adoptions, is selling organs to hospitals for medical transplants. For Guatemalans who have endured decades of state-backed terror supported by the United States, Flor's crimes do not seem far-fetched: "Guatemala, three decades of war, the overall effects of that, a pretty lawless place where all sorts of ordinarily questionable acts might seem justified by practical necessity" (60–61). Rogerio even justifies Flor's alleged crimes, suggesting that one could engage in illegal adoption as a means of expediting a process. These accusations are made within the context of a civil society under siege by a corrupt and murderous government as well as foreign entities with blood on their hands, such that even a crime such as baby selling or organ trafficking seems possible.

Moya is another character through whom the novel broaches the history of U.S. intervention in the region. Although he is well aware of the role of the United States in Guatemalan economic and military affairs, he himself cannot avoid close associations with U.S. officials, some of whom provide him with much-needed assistance. In this way Moya reflects the complicated relationship between Guatemala and the United States in which the latter has both contributed to violence and instability in the former while also providing assistance and refugee for individual Guatemalans. Moya's character and in particular his close relationship with the political science professor Sylvia McCourt allows readers insight into close ties between U.S. and Guatemalan political and military leaders. Moya tells Rogerio that he met McCourt at a party thrown by the press attaché of the U.S. embassy. Also present were Moya's boss, the media tycoon Celso Batres, as well as members of the Guatemalan armed forces and several other owners of newspapers in Guatemala. While this scene elucidates the ties between government and media workers in Guatemala, characters also reference the role of the United States. In a clumsy attempt to flirt, Colonel Lenz, the head of the Guatemalan Army's press relations tells Dr. McCourt that she is "more beautiful than Jeane Kirkpatrick" (271). The comment may be both humorous and upsetting as it invokes a conservative political figure whose policies and views were incredibly damaging to Central America and Guatemala. An ardent anticommunist and a member of Ronald Reagan's cabinet, Kirkpatrick is well remembered for the doctrine that bears her name, which asserted that the United States could work with "authoritarian" regimes and dictators to establish democracy. Her idea held that such regimes were preferable to "totalitarian" (that is, left-leaning, communist, or socialist) ones and was used to justify support for right-wing governments in El Salvador and Guatemala.[36] Lenz's comment indicates his own, and by extension the Guatemalan Army's, familiarity with Kirkpatrick and thus the close relationship between the Guatemalan military and right-wing U.S. politicians.

The United States however also provides a safe haven for people such as Moya. Referred to by Rogerio as "the country's last truly independent print journalist," Moya possesses an independence that has a price, and he eventually has to flee to the United States (293). His friendship with U.S. citizens such as Dr. McCourt allows him access to a fellowship at Harvard, where he spends six months. Moya's time in the States also enables him to befriend more people who can help guarantee his safety: "He has many more influential and powerful connections now. Profs who can phone profs who can phone distinguished alumni senators and ambassadors who can phone *generalísimos* and say: Let that boy go!" (109). Characters such as Moya and Flor permit the novel to explicate the long-standing and complicated relationship between the United States and Guatemala in which the former has helped fund murderous counterinsurgency campaigns while also providing a safe haven for people fleeing that very same violence.

State of Impunity: Collusion among Government, Military, and Media

While the United States has unquestionably played a large role in Guatemala's violent past, *The Long Night of White Chickens* also addresses Guatemala's internal crime and corruption. The state of impunity that reigns throughout the text is often illustrated through the relationship between government, military, and media actors who allow each other to cover up their crimes. The guests of the party where Moya meets Dr. McCourt, mentioned above, speaks to the close ties between U.S. and Guatemalan political workers and Guatemalan media. Moya tells readers of the political aspirations of Batres and other newspaper owners who hope to use their fame and power to occupy the presidential palace. These aspirations come with the acknowledgment that such a position would have to be sanctioned by the army and involve "passively [presiding] over so many lucrative rackets, so as not to alienate [their] democratic allies in the army high command" (268). Rather than hold government and military actors accountable for their crimes, these media men aspire to become part of a government that is itself kept in check by the powerful military.

While Rogerio is aware of the corruption and impunity within Guatemala, Moya and their friendship open his eyes to media complicity. At one point Moya exasperatingly explains to Rogerio what a *fafero* is. Surprised that his friend is not familiar with the term, the former exclaims: "It's a reporter who takes *fafas, vos*-bribes" (229). Moya explains that *faferos* were possibly paid to attribute an illegal adoption house run by someone else (with ties to the military) to Flor; thus *faferos* hinder and complicate Rogerio's investigations into Flor's death while simultaneously protecting corrupt individuals. The novel never goes into detail about any individual *fafero,* but the frequent and offhand references to *faferos* suggest that such journalists are indeed a large proportion of the Guatemalan press. That they are almost always discussed in the plural, *faferos,* further contributes to a portrait of rampant corruption and collusion within the nation.

While he distinguishes himself from *faferos,* Moya is nevertheless part of an industry whose work is compromised by its relationship with government and business leaders. This relationship is illustrated in the character of Celso Batres, Moya's boss, and the owner of several newspapers. Rogerio explains: "Moya writes for *El Minuto,* a low-circulation broadsheet of never more than twelve pages . . . but [the Batres family] really makes their money from *Dónde?* by far the most popular 'newspaper' in the country, . . . and the Batres name appears nowhere in its pages" (176). Later Goldman's characteristic humor is used to offer another perspective on the various qualities of Guatemala City newspapers: "to say that [*Dónde?* is a Guatemalan version of] *The National*

Enquirer is definitely an offense to the editorial standards of the latter" (176). In fact, Moya also occasionally and strategically writes for *Dónde?* When the reporter oversteps his boundaries and receives death threats, Batres sends Moya to write under a pseudonym at *Dónde?* until things blow over. Moya thus benefits from Batres' considerable wealth and reach.

In addition to a U.S.-backed military and bribe-taking journalists, *The Long Night of White Chickens* also points to Guatemalan police as contributing to impunity. Rogerio, watching the city move past him from his spot at a local coffee shop, describes Guatemala City as "the urban capital of a well-entrenched police state" (15). The novel names actual police officers, including the head of the National Police, Germán Chupina Barahona. Better known as Chupina, he served as head of the National Police under Romeo Lucas García, years that coincide with the time period of the novel as well as some of the bloodiest years in Guatemala's history. While the police who investigate Flor's death are not implicated in her murder, their conduct does not help to solve the crime or to suggest their own integrity. Rogerio explains that many of Flor's personal items have gone "missing" from her room, although he somewhat sympathetically quips that such is to be expected from "police who don't even earn a hundred bucks a month" (98). The somewhat benign crimes of such police alongside the pointed mention of Chupina allow Rogerio to acknowledge a culture of criminality while distinguishing between large- and small-scale actors.

Humor and Repetition

The title of Marc Zimmerman's article on the novel, "Woody Allen visita [visits] Guatemala," clearly points to the role of humor in the text, a humor that Zimmerman, by invoking the name of the well-known Jewish American comedian, suggested is perhaps similarly and specifically Jewish American. The humor in *The Long Night of White Chickens* is less self-obsessed and neurotic than that for which Allen is well known, but it is intelligent and politically informed. Goldman himself has expressed amazement at those who fail to see the humor in his work, remarking in an interview with Caleb Bach that he has been "baffled" when a reader or review does not see the humor in his writing, adding that "humor is one of [his] crucial tools."[37]

Two aspects of the novel's humor are remarkable: its darkness and its self-referentiality. The darkness comes out when Rogerio and other characters make jokes about things such as government-backed violence and the poverty of Guatemala. For example, Rogerio explains that he'd lost touch with his childhood friend Moya but reconnected with him in 1979, "on the unforgettably chaotic day that the government reversed the direction of all the major one-way avenues in Guatemala City" (6). Throughout the rest of the chapter, Rogerio's narrative moves between the present and several pasts: his childhood decades ago, his trip to Guatemala to recover Flor's body a year ago, and his renewed connection with Moya several months ago. But he continues referring to the afternoon in 1979 and always through the same description, saying in that same chapter that he ran into Moya "the day they [the government] reversed the direction of the one-way traffic." And later, "That day five years ago, when the government changed the direction of the one-way traffic on the city's major avenues, Moya was right here in Pastelería Hemmings, sitting at a table with three other student types" (13, 15). The effect of this repetition is to create a memory for the reader so that by the second and third invocation, we ourselves remember it from its earlier mention and are drawn into Rogerio's world, where his memories literally come ours.

Of course the content of the description is ludicrous and brings to mind a callous and dangerous government. Moya wryly comments on one of the results of the change in direction: ten people have died so far as a result of the change in traffic patterns, through accidents or by being run over. Moya quips: "Permit me to say that as a way of relieving traffic congestion I find this not bad. Eliminate the drivers, eliminate the pedestrians" (16). Moya distinguishes himself from other characters in his sharp assessments of Guatemalan society and government, offering pointed critiques that use dark humor to describe the culture and society. Later in the novel readers learn that Moya was offered a job at *El Minuto* after speaking up during a question-and-answer session hosted by his university and featuring Batres. The young man, at the time a university student, commented: "here in Guatemala there is a fundamental respect for freedom of expression. Here, anyone is free to say whatever he wants. And if someone doesn't like it, then he's free to kill you" (253). Moya's pointed statements offer insight into the state of affairs in Guatemala while bringing dark humor to the text. We may view Moya's perspective as a particularly Latin American one in his well-founded cynicism that is nevertheless overruled by a sense of hope and the determination to pursue justice.

Just as jokes about traffic patterns are repeated, so too do references to specific and phrases and events occur throughout the novel. Rogerio often refers to specific memories several times. These include the summer of 1979, when he drove to Guatemala to visit Flor; Flor and Moya's "long night of white chickens"; and Rogerio's encounter with a food truck, knishes *chapín*, in Boston.[38] The near-continuous back-and-forth references create the feeling that the novel covers a much larger time period than it does; in fact the vast majority of the narrative's events occur within four years (1979–83). In all cases these repetitions create a seemingly autonomous world within the novel, where characters' memories become that of the readers.

In Summation

According to Goldman *The Long Night of White Chickens* was written "to save [his] own life! . . . to grow more, to know more, to bring [his] two worlds together."[39] The extended engagement with Guatemalan American characters as well as Guatemalan politics and government in the early 1980s reflects Goldman bringing his own background and worlds to bear on his writing. Furthermore, the role of journalism and specifically the character of Moya illustrate Goldman's experience as a journalist and his appreciation for long-form journalism. Still fiction offered a particular way of sorting through experiences emerging from the "horrible morass of politics" he had encountered while living in Guatemala and ultimately providing a "life-affirming" process.[40] The humor that we see throughout the text is likewise a means of affirmation, a way of confronting the brutal reality of Guatemala's civil war while asserting that survivors have not forgotten the crimes of the regime. In the publication of this remarkable first novel Goldman succeeded in saving his own life and establishing his as a major voice within U.S. literature.

CHAPTER 3

Movement and Memory in *The Ordinary Seaman*

Just five years after the publication of *The Long Night of White Chickens,* Goldman published *The Ordinary Seaman.* Focusing on a crew of Central American laborers brought to the Brooklyn harbor to live and work on a boat that never sails, the novel touches on issues of labor, migration, globalization, and stagnation and struck a nerve with a wide range of readers. *The Ordinary Seaman* is a book in which readers can find many different stories, depending on what they are looking for. For those interested in history, Goldman has retold an event that occurred in 1982, creating memorable characters and life histories to grant depth and humanity to a story that he originally encountered in a newspaper. Critics of globalization may find in the text sharp assessments of this new age of transnationalism wherein capital and power can move relatively unencumbered, and even unrecognized, while the bodies of the poor remain confined, overlooked, and ignored. Of course the text also contains its literary and mythical references; as the majority of the narrative takes place on a boat, the work has elicited comparisons to the work of Herman Melville, while others have noted its Borgian structure and the Sisyphean work to which the crew are assigned. In addition, the text, like all of Goldman's work, retains ethnic and national particularities such that it remains specifically concerned with the lives of Central American characters and how they fare in relation to the United States.

The Ordinary Seaman tells the story of a group of Central American men who have signed on to work on a ship, the *Urus.* Unbeknownst to them the ship is part of an attempted scheme by its co-owners, Elias Tureen and Mark Baker. Elias, the son of a British father and Greek American mother, who was raised in Mexico City, is the smooth-talking visionary of the plan. He puts together a business scheme with his best friend, the Anglo-American Mark. The two met in college in upstate New York, and years later Elias convinces Mark to invest money he has inherited after his father's death into buying an old ship. According to Elias the "easiest way to make money with a ship like this one . . . was to fix her up cheap, insure her for much more money than you'd paid, and sink her" (298–99). But the two are never able to bring the boat to a functioning condition, largely owing to the ship's outdated equipment. "It had never occurred to Elias that it would turn out to be nearly impossible to find replacement circuit breakers for a circa 1970 made-in-Japan generator" (278). While the two owners slowly come to terms with this reality, the crew are left to "work" on the *Urus*. They spend months tinkering with electrical equipment, cleaning and repainting the ship while fighting off rats who threaten their meager food supply and trying to fortify themselves against the increasingly cold New York weather. Death permeates the men's existence: they work on a mechanically dead ship, their unpaid labor evokes slave ships, and their lack of proper paperwork mean they exist in a state of social death, unrecognized by any state.[1] Elias and Mark visit the ship on seemingly random occasions, bringing a few modest supplies and assuring the crew that they will be compensated for their work once they themselves are. The two owners maintain an elaborate ruse, encouraging the men to keep a log of their hours worked and even offering them all promotions. After the tragic death of one of the crew, which he is convinced will finally draw attention the slave ship he has been running, Mark abandons the enterprise and absconds to Cancún. Elias, who was careful never to put any paperwork in his own name, instead making sure everything was signed by Achuar Corporation, only has to disconnect the answering machine he has set up to handle any phone calls for his shipping company to walk away from the project. In the meantime, the men manage to make contact with a Seafarer's Institute, which helps them file a legal complaint and offers them some shelter as well as airfare to their native countries. But by this time, one of the crew has started a life off the boat and among the Latina/o immigrant community in Brooklyn; rather than return home penniless and humiliated, the majority of the surviving crew decide to remain in New York and quietly join the undocumented community of the city.

Among the group of fifteen, who come from Nicaragua, Honduras, and Guatemala, two men rise to a position of leadership, and the narrative focuses on their lives on and off the boat, in the past and the present. Esteban Gaitan is a nineteen-year-old veteran of the Contra War in Nicaragua who served in an elite guerilla Sandinista battalion, a BLI (Batallón de Lucha Irregular, Irregular Fighting Unit), where he witnessed many compatriots and his young love,

Marta, murdered by U.S.-backed Contra soldiers. Bernardo, also Nicaraguan, is the oldest member of the crew and the only to have served at sea; he is the ship's waiter. Although he is often dismissed by others, particularly Esteban, who unsuccessfully attempts to avoid developing a father-son relationship with the *viejo* (old man), Bernado is the only seaman who accurately and consistently names their predicament. The day they board the *Urus,* Bernardo looks out across the Brooklyn harbor at the Statue of Liberty and declares, "When that statue walks, chavalos [kids], this ship will sail" (45).

The *Urus* is docked in a remote area of the Brooklyn harbor, just adjacent to public housing projects. As Capitán Elias informs them, they have documentation only to allow them to work on the boat, thus they cannot legally set foot on shore. For Jennifer Harford Vargas this situation makes the *Urus* a "floating dictator-ship," literally afloat in the Brooklyn waterfront and figuratively afloat between U.S. and Latin American territory and history.[2] Not only the ship but its inhabitants exist in a liminal space.[3] Despite Elias's warning after less than a week on board, the crew try their luck on land and endure a humiliating beating and robbery at the hands of *los* blacks, African American residents of the nearby Red Hook projects.[4] The incident, validating Elias's ability to accurately predict sources of danger, contributes to the crew's feelings of isolation and impotence and seemingly unreasonable deference to their boss.

Bernardo and Esteban contribute the most to the novel's story line as well as to the crew's eventual, although incomplete, salvation. Washing himself at a spigot on the pier one afternoon, Bernardo encounters an elderly Argentinian couple looking for a man they heard lived on the pier. Bernardo pleads with them to inform someone of the crew's predicament, and the couple's report eventually makes its way to the Seafarer's Institute where a "Ship Visitor," John, is assigned to the case and makes contact with the abandoned crew. John's job as ship visitor involves boarding ships to assess the situation of those working on board; his job is made difficult by the inherently transitory nature of the industry he inspects: often a ship is setting sail before he can provide much assistance. The *Urus,* however, poses a different set of problems. By the time John arrives, the ship's owners have failed to pay taxes, meaning that the ship is now unregistered and the men unprotected by the laws of any country. Moreover, because Elias never gave the crew shipping articles to sign, they have never been legally employed, making their case against Elias and Mark weaker.

Although Bernardo is integral to their discovery by John, he does not live to join the others in surviving their ordeal. While preparing rice he suffers a burn from cooking oil. Elias, who is trained in homeopathic remedies, treats Bernardo, but his wound becomes infected. While Elias is in Los Angeles scouring shipyards for a replacement circuit breaker, Mark drives Bernardo to a Manhattan hospital, hoping the distance from Brooklyn will at least impede the ability of authorities to connect the injured man with the others left on board. Mark literally dumps Bernardo in the emergency room and then leaves. Bernardo dies soon after and is buried in a cemetery for indigents, Potter's Field on Hart Island. Mark clears out his apartment and flees the country.

Meanwhile Esteban, encouraged by Bernardo, has begun to make forays into Brooklyn. He wanders the streets at night, looking for supplies that may be useful to the crew. He sneaks into warehouses and onto the back of delivery trucks, stealing a carton before he has a chance to look at its contents. As a result, he brings back a mixed bag of goods: a case of Parcheesi games, men's underwear in size XL, swimming goggles; but he also happens upon bags of frozen shrimp (labeled, ironically, from Honduras) as well as the leg of a cow. Esteban insists on going alone and early one morning happens upon a manicurist opening the salon where she works. He sweeps the shop in exchange for a cup of coffee, and the two become friends and eventually lovers. Joaquína, an undocumented immigrant from Mexico, introduces Esteban to the Latina/o immigrant world of Brooklyn. Her boss, Gonzalo, a gay former ballet dancer from Cuba who was exiled from that country along with thousands of others during the Mariel Boat Lift, is warm and welcoming to Esteban. Gonzalo allows Esteban to sleep in the salon, cuts his hair, and acquires him secondhand clothes so that he is able to look for work. Through a fellow Nicaraguan he meets at a salsa club, Esteban is hired to work at a chair factory run by a Colombian, where he earns $2 an hour. He mostly continues to sleep on the ship and uses his salary to maintain the crew while also saving some so that he and Joaquína may someday rent their own apartment. For Marta Caminero-Santangelo, Esteban's work to provide for the crew indicates that the novel is one that is diasporic, rather than transnational. When he returns to the ship with provisions, the *Urus* becomes "back home" for Esteban, indicating that his horizontal allegiance to other diasporic peoples has superseded any ties to another nation.[5] Indeed, whether or not the characters retain firm ties to their nations of origin, few return there in the course of the novel. When winter comes and the Seafarer's Institute moves quickly to offer the crew passage home, Esteban accepts the offers of help he has received from other immigrants and secures lodging for the men who wish to try their luck in New York. Only a handful of the crew return to Central America via the Seafarer's Institute, two who choose to do so and four others who have taken to sniffing paint solvents and are largely unreliable and incoherent. The cook, who claims he is too old to immigrate, explains to the confused ship visitor that Esteban "has friends in the city who've offered to put them all up for a while. The drug addicts wanted to go too, but Esteban wouldn't take them, pues [well], He said he couldn't do that to his friends in the city" (381).

While the end of *The Ordinary Seaman* offers some resolution for the crew, their captors are never brought to justice. This lack of punishment mimics the case on which Goldman based his book. In his acknowledgments, Goldman explained that a 1982 *New York Daily News* article about seventeen abandoned sailors was the inspiration for the novel. He had just arrived in New York and was able to speak to some of the crew who were housed at the Seamen's Church Institute in Manhattan. The waiter, Bernardo Iván Carrasco M., made such an impression on the author that he named the *Urus's* waiter after him. The story remained with Goldman for over a decade, and in 1995, "feeling a bit shipwrecked in [his] own life," Goldman finally sat down to write the novel (383). His work was really able to take off, however, after he was able to spend a month on board a ship that sailed from Mexico to Barcelona. In the time that Goldman was researching and writing, a book about the abuses against mariners was published, *Trouble on Board: The Plight of International Seafarers* (Cornell University Press, 1992). The author, Rev. Paul Chapman, covered the case on which the *Urus* is based and explained that the ship's owners escaped prosecution. The owners managed to auction off but then repurchase their own ship and attempted to repeat their scam at least two more times.

While the story of the *Urus* and its crew is remarkable enough, Goldman's writing style and commitment to deep storytelling transcend the particulars of the case. Critics lauded the text's timely story line and empathy for its characters. Robert Houston of the *New York Times* commended Goldman's ability to construct a nonlinear storyline and invoked Walt Whitman by writing that the novel "contains multitudes."[6] Sybil Steinberg of *Publisher's Weekly* found the additional story lines, which go into detail about Esteban's experiences in the war, the ship visitor's relationship with his girlfriend Ariadne, and Elias and Mark's friendship in college, risked "[impeding] the narrative's forward movement" but that they eventually came together "into a searing picture of human vulnerability and courage."[7] Houston, too, found the text's treatment of its individual characters noteworthy; "Goldman," the critic wrote, "often satirizes, [but] never stoops to condescension."[8] These reviews capture some of the fundamental contradictions at the heart of the novel—between stasis and movement and between people and processes.

Despite focusing on a ship that never moves, *The Ordinary Seaman* sails through several important literary and political discussions. As alluded to earlier, the time of publication in the late 1990s, and its setting in the late 1980s (Esteban hears of the fall of the Berlin Wall on a radio), allow the novel to comment on significant moments of change. In fact, the text explicitly *questions* change, movement, and progress. The opening sentence of the novel describes

Esteban arriving at the Managua airport to begin his journey to the United States. However, when he arrives, the airport is closed. Only later do readers understand that this (temporarily) aborted journey foreshadows the one that is to come aboard the *Urus* and the larger lack of movement that marks Esteban's life in the United States. A later section describes Esteban's meditation on lack of movement in a temporal sense, questioning the relationship between futurity, progress, and movement. After delving into memories of the Contra War the young man declares: "They were always telling you that the war was over the future, no? . . . And now the future is here and, hijueputa, look at it: a ship that doesn't move" (177). For April Shemak, Esteban's reluctance to share his memories of the war with the other crew reflects a kind of anti-*testimonio* in which the impetus and outcome of the *testimonio,* a text meant to narrate the coming to consciousness of a political actor and the establishing of solidarity between writer and reader, is inverted.[9] Esteban and the other characters question what is new or desirable about the future, simultaneously invoking the futility of war as well as capitalist development, economic expansion, and global integration. When John the ship visitor is able to name the ship for what is, a slave ship, the novel recalls the transatlantic slave trade, further connecting contemporary modes of confinement and exploitation with past ones and again suggesting that little has changed.

According to Rodrigo Lazo, *The Ordinary Seaman* is a "hemispheric novel" because it calls attention "to complex settings that include people from various parts of the hemisphere who negotiate power imbalances that have roots in the colonial history of the Americas."[10] The critic explained that slavery was often a central concern of the hemispheric American novel of the nineteenth century, while migration and globalization are more often found in its contemporary form. Goldman's novel, however, is also often concerned with the relationship between slavery and migration, suggesting that these are not necessarily discrete conditions. Likewise, the work challenges readers to draw connections between seemingly disparate ideas and processes, including movement and stasis, wage labor and slavery, and immigration and exile. *The Ordinary Seaman* engages with transnational issues—transnational migration, transnational labor, transnational Latina/o peoples and experiences—asking us to look simultaneously at movement between and among national and political contexts as well as between the past, present, and future. The adjective "trans" can be further welded to several themes in the novel: temporality, labor, *Latinidad,* and the transition between life and death. All four require deeper scrutiny and the kind of sustained attention that only a story about a ship that never sails can provide.

Transtemporality

Several critics have focused on the novel's preoccupation with time as a means to think through issues of temporality and circularity within U.S. letters and history. The novel weaves the preoccupation with time throughout nearly the entire book with its frequent use of the present anterior tense. Several chapters are written entirely in this tense. Describing the outcome of Bernardo's contact with the Argentinian couple, readers are told: "In another six weeks, in December, after a night of freezing rain, the Ship Visitor will find them. He'll board a ship whose name and port of registration will have recently been painted off the prow and stern" (129). While this particular passage suggests the beginning of the end, that is, the end of the crew's ordeal aboard the *Urus,* its occurrence less than halfway through the novel suggests that the end—or the future—has not yet arrived. As readers we know that we, and the crew, have much more to go through before arriving at this moment. At the same time the novel's cynicism about the resolution of the future requires that we temper any hope concerning this passage.

For Kirsten Silva Gruesz the text's preoccupation with the relationship between the past, present, and future refers to significant twentieth-century thinkers similarly focused on temporality. She explained that *The Ordinary Seaman* calls to mind philosophers such as Walter Benjamin and Ernst Bloch who argued for the necessity of a theory of history. (Gruesz, "Utopia Latina," 57) The novel invokes these earlier thinkers while offering U.S. Latina/o perspectives, specifically by writing U.S. influence into the history of Latin American peoples and nations. This influence comes out via the men's stories about their lives in Central America. While Esteban confronted U.S. military power through his fighting against the CIA-backed Contras, others frequently encountered U.S. economic intervention. Caratumba from Guatemala recalls working for a U.S. oil exploration company. When these men are forced to seek out opportunities in the United States, the novel offers a circular historical perspective on U.S. influence in which the past of U.S. intervention becomes the present of migrants in the United States.

These ruminations on the ways in which the U.S. past has created the U.S. present have particular implications for U.S. Latina/os. As Gruesz pointed out, Latina/os are often referenced through a particular temporal grammar and the use of the present progressive tense, for example, "Latina/os are becoming the largest minority" (Ibid., 55) Michael Templeton used similar language, calling the Latina/o community that Esteban joins one that is "in a state of becoming."[11] Such language reveals as much as it conceals, bringing visibility to this supposedly "emerging" population within the United States while often failing to account for the long history of Latina/os in the United States or for communities that remain marginalized and invisible (that is, the undocumented). This investment in the language of revelation and concealment is undertaken by the U.S. government and media as well as Latina/o studies scholars themselves, leading Gruesz to suggest that the field itself needs a philosophy of history. According to Gruesz *The Ordinary Seaman* intervenes in this conundrum by being a historical novel, albeit one completely lacking in historical characters. Rather what makes *The Ordinary Seaman* a historical novel is the characters' own understanding "that the present moment they occupy *is* historical time." (Gruesz, "Utopia Latina," 58)

The crew of the *Urus* spend their days and nights thinking about their lives before this ordeal and what will happen after. In their sleep they often travel to other times and places, alluding to pre-Colombian cosmologies of night that entail a belief that the soul travels while one sleeps.[12] Nevertheless they remain concerned with the present and specifically with the passage of, and marking of, time. Several crew members brought clocks with them, but only two of them are battery operated and able to run on the electricity-less ship. When one of these clocks is destroyed by a cat who appears and remains for several weeks, the men decide to guard their remaining timepiece in a safe location, the food locker. "Whenever anyone wanted to know what time it was, he had to go to the food locker, yank with all his strength on the handle until the door opened in a burst of hot, rancid air and flaky debris, and there was the clock, on the rotted wood-planked floor, loudly ticking away, phosphorescent green hands and numerals faintly glowing in the dark" (85). When the clock's hour hand goes missing, rendering it useless, the men are dismayed and accuse one another until Elias points out that the hand was probably taken by one of the ship's numerous rats, who coveted the shiny piece for a nest. The destruction of the clock plunges the men into an unmarked existence, increasing their reliance on the comings and goings of Elias and Mark, who occasionally bring a radio with them, but never leave it behind.

Once the last clock is destroyed, only one timepiece remains on board, a Mickey Mouse watch that Esteban was given by his late lover and which he guards obsessively. Sometimes, when Esteban is alone in the cabin and is sure that Bernardo is busy in the mess or with some other chore, he reaches into his suitcase and pulls out the dirty green sock in which he keeps the watch. The watch remains on central time; Esteban never bothers to adjust it to New York time and often simply touches the watch through the sock, remembering the woman who gave it to him. Although Esteban's watch continues to mark time, life on the boat for the men remains stagnant. The one functioning timepiece thus serves as a counterpoint to the men's suspension in time and space. As

María DeGuzmán pointed out, clocks become a metaphor to describe grief; the men ruminate on time as they ruminate on their losses. (Ibid., 173) Rather than passing or moving, time fills the men "like the stagnant air in a flourishing mushroom cellar" (38).

Suspended in a state of timelessness and statelessness, the *Urus* nevertheless evokes times and places from other moments in U.S. history and literature. The text naturally elicits comparisons to the work of Herman Melville and has sparked new conversations about Melville and his critics. While the ship may provoke comparisons to *Moby Dick's Pequod,* several critics have suggested that it is *Benito Cereno's Saint Dominick,* a slave ship, that is the more apt comparison. When Mark thinks to himself that he is the owner of slave ship, the text questions the temporal markings of slavery; as Gruesz asked: "what is the connection between the *historical* trauma of enslavement and the *contemporary* trade in the labor power of the very poor, with its highest cost in displaced lives?"[13] Not only are the uncompensated laborers linked spatiotemporally; so are those who benefit. Ana Patricia Rodríguez suggested that the text calls readers to place themselves in relation, as "everyday [consumers linked] to the greater flow of capital and division and exploitation of Third World labor."[14] Goldman's book builds off a distinctly U.S. literary preoccupation with maritime worlds while offering a cynical update, paying particular attention to the fate of those exploited by the quest for power and capital.

Transnational Labor and Migration

The Ordinary Seaman is undoubtedly a novel about exploited, vulnerable labor, and the work provides rich thought for investigation into contemporary and past forms of uncompensated work. Angela Naimou looked at "modes of salvage" in the text, explicating how salvage work manipulates or reveals states of exceptional personhood. She read the novel in light of a significant nineteenth-century court case, *Robertson v. Baldwin,* which ruled that merchant marines who challenged their status could be held liable for criminal charges.[15] For her the abandoned crew are circumscribed not only because their immigrant status, but also because of ideas (logics) and laws about free, laboring subjects. The "legally unfree laborer," she argued, is juxtaposed not to the free laborer, but to the ship and corporate person. Both the unfree laborer and the corporation occupy a position of exceptional personhood. In this reading ships play an important role, standing in for a sovereign power.

For Rick Moody, who reviewed the book for the *Los Angeles Times,* Goldman's exposé of maritime exploitation is akin to Upton Sinclair's revelations concerning factory work in *The Jungle.* Moody described the novel as "a sort of anti-imperialist, post-colonial, democratic, culturally multifarious novel of the sea."[16] The text also recalls transnational writers who have explored the sea as a site of confinement and liberation. Naimou and Gruesz both argued that *The Ordinary Seaman* can be understood in relation to C. L. R. James's 1953 work *Mariners, Renegades and Castaways: The Story of Herman Melville and the World We Live In*. The conditions under which Trinidadian-born James wrote the book, while he was imprisoned on Ellis Island, connect both artists and their work to questions of captivity and freedom in the maritime world. From this perspective the crew of the *Urus* are not an entirely new kind of exploited class; they are linked to centuries of maritime and other laborers who have been systematically excluded by nation-specific laws while exploited by transnational corporations.

Naimou also analyzed the designation of the men as "ordinary seamen." In fact they are legally akin to slaves, wage laborers, economic migrants, unauthorized refugees, and aliens.[17] This distinction points out the range of classifications beyond the binary of "free" or "unfree" laborer while also linking the crew to those held captive on the slave ships of the transatlantic slave trade. Furthermore, when courts ruled that seamen were "an exceptional class of men" whose rights were distinct than that of other laborers, they placed them in a position similar to other racialized peoples. Deemed necessary to the nation and yet outside its legal protections, the law constructed seamen as childlike people who needed others to make decisions to protect them.[18] The co-owner of the *Urus* Mark uses similar language to refer to the crew. Toward the end of the narrative, when Mark is increasingly disillusioned and frustrated with both Elias and their entire scheme, he thinks about the crew as "our little brown guys" (305). He refers to himself as "First Mate Mark Pizarro" and his co-conspirator as "Capitán Elias Cortés," linking them to centuries of racialized conquest and colonization, or in Naimou's words, "haunting imperial and natural traces."[19] But he remains fixated on the present and the links between the "little brown men" aboard the *Urus* and those he encounters in New York City. He remains resentful for "being reminded, of feeling angry and guilty everywhere he goes, that's all, because everywhere he goes he sees them: busboys, McDonald's, even working in pizza parlors now instead of Italians and Greeks" (305). When Mark finally admits to himself that what he owns is a slave ship, he does what the crew and readers have already done and belatedly connects different forms of unfree labor across several centuries and continents.

For Harford Vargas the text forms part of a larger oeuvre of Latina/o "dictatorship novels" with Elias and Mark serving as the despotic agents of the narrative. The owners' power is directly related to the historical, political, and economic moment in which the work is set such that the neoliberal, post–Cold War economy allows the two men to take advantage of the neoliberal free market and emerge as "phantom dictators."[20] Harford Vargas's analysis, like that of Naimou's, concentrates on the ship as a site of exploitation, domination, and control. She argued that the ship itself is a "floating authoritarian space" grounded in hierarchical relations. Looking at the multiple meanings of the term "discourse," which encapsulates both the idea of a narrative and a plotted course, as well as a larger history of shipwreck narratives within Western literature (including for instance *The Odyssey, Gulliver's Travels, Moby Dick*), the critic suggested that *The Ordinary Seaman* is a shipwreck narrative in which the wrecked *Urus* signals its own material state as well as "the dark underside of imperial designs." (Ibid., 90, 104) Despite their disempowered relationship to their rulers, Harford Vargas argued that the survivors of the *Urus* shipwreck are eventually able to piece together an existence through the "holes and scraps" of their situation. These scraps are social as well as material and include the larger community of refugees and exiles that Esteban encounters in New York City. Thus we may even view Latina/o immigrants and exiles as survivors of social and economic shipwrecks who nonetheless work with, in Naimou's word, "salvage" elements to construct new lives.

The exploitation of labor that is at the center of the novel means that *The Ordinary Seaman* engages in a continued questioning of what is new or laudable about contemporary forms of commerce, culture, and language. Furthermore, in examining transnational connections, the text also questions the idea of the nation and national cohesion. According to Templeton "the idea that a nation can consist as a cohesive singular entity is challenged" by transnational communities that drive home the necessity of a new language to capture a "highly mobile and technologically connected world." (Templeton, "Become Transnational," 271) The text achieves this portrait not by eliding national differences, but by exploring them, thereby drawing attention to "the molecular conditions" that lay beneath transnational immigrant experiences (Ibid., 279). The particular lives and histories of the crew as well as the *Urus*'s owners suggest that a "transnational" culture or experience is not one that supersedes individual nationalistic ones, but one that contains them. These experiences, however, are not contained in an even or uniform way as the extremely asymmetric boundaries of power between the characters who possess U.S. citizenship and those who do not are driven home.

Transnational Latinidad

Goldman was unabashed at placing the men's stories, rather than that of their exploiters or the nameless and faceless progenitors of power, at the forefront of his narrative. This favoring of the crew led Moody to lament that Mark and Elias lack "the complex psychologizing or remorseful conquest of" other literary captains and to remark that their characters are "without the moral verisimilitude of their Central American counterparts."[21] This was clearly the intent of the novel. Again *The Ordinary Seaman*'s literary predecessor is more *Benito Cereno,* with its explorations of relations of power, race, and captivity, than *Moby Dick*. Goldman was less interested in exploring the psychological world of his villains, those already profiting from the privileges their citizenship, race, and education afford them. But it bears mentioning that *The Ordinary Seaman* is interested in the lives of not only immigrants and laborers but specifically Central American migrants. The men come from three countries—Nicaragua, Guatemala, and Honduras. These three nations have experienced the impacts of U.S. military and economic policies in its "backyard"; Guatemala and Honduras (along with El Salvador) are part of the Northern Triangle of Central America that sends thousands of migrants to the United States every year. Aboard the ship the men, despite deep differences in race, age, and life experience, form a cohesive unit that speaks to the experience of racialization that migrants undergo within the United States. That is to say, migrants from nations that may see themselves as having very little in common say, Mexico and Nicaragua, often find themselves occupying similar social positions in the United States. Because of redlining and segregation in housing and labor markets, such migrants often find themselves living in the same neighborhoods and working in similar industries. Together with linguistic, national, or racial discrimination they may face, this creates a commonality of experience where before there may have been very little. In effect U.S. racial policies create racial identities; treated as "foreign Latinos," these migrants, despite initial ways of thinking about themselves and identifying, may take on that very same identity category.

In Goldman's book this process of racial formation through neglect and marginalization happens in a condensed and extreme manner. The men are forced to become a cohesive unit, and whatever differences due to age, race, nationality, life experience, or any combination of these may have marked them before their ordeal on the *Urus,* they are now indelibly marked by their collective experience. They have formed a unit that distinguishes them from both *los blacks* of *los proyectos* (the blacks of the projects) as well as the Latina/os that Esteban encounters in Brooklyn. Here the book demonstrates how experiences of racial, linguistic, and economic marginalization and discrimination actually *create* the sort of specific identity, in this case Latina/o or Central American, that such policies assume to already exist. As the novel focuses exclusively on Central Americans, Goldman has suggested that a coherent Central American or Central American–American identity may likewise have just as much to do with the impacts of U.S. imperial and military policies as with any "natural" links between the nations and their peoples. A Guatemalan American writer himself, Goldman has admitted that what drew him to the true story of the abandoned ship on which the book is based was the Central American origins of the crew. He demonstrates in this and all his novels his specific interest in granting visibility to, and narrating the complexities of, Central American and Central American–American identities and experiences.

At the same time, when Esteban meets Joaquína and assimilates into Brooklyn Latina/o life, we see the breadth and porousness of a larger subset of U.S. Latina/o and immigrant identities. In New York Esteban encounters a Latina/o language that he does not understand, even while he recognizes it as Spanish. Wandering through Brooklyn he notes: "Sometimes the tiendas' [stores'] signs are in Spanish—what does *Quisqueya* mean?" (196). He recognizes the word as one with a Spanish origin but cannot divine its meaning. Quisqueya refers to the island of Quisqueyana, the indigenous name of the island now known as Hispaniola and divided into two countries, Haiti and the Dominican Republic. A similar linguistic barrier marks Esteban's first encounter with Joaquína. Joaquína speaks with a heavy reliance on slang, referring to Esteban as "*güey*" and ending sentences with "órale," neither of which Esteban understands. Her language marks her as Mexican and specifically *chilanga,* someone from Mexico City (in fact she is from the nearby state of Zacatecas but attended school in the capital). Esteban resists Joaquína when she addresses him as *güey,* a word commonly used among familiar people, similar to the English "dude" or "man": "But my name isn't *güey,* its Esteban" (215). Joaquína's language reflects the extent to which immigrants in the United States "maintain a sense of their original nationality."[22] Rather than suggest that Joaquína is the only character who speaks with a nationally inflected accent, Goldman has pointed out that Esteban speaks a specifically Nicaraguan form of Spanish. Joaquína says to him, "You have a funny accent. . . . What's all that with *vos*?" (212). Esteban explains that he is from Nicaragua, one of several countries in Latin America (others include Argentina and El Salvador) that use *vos* in place of the familiar "you" form, *tú.* These exchanges alert readers to the multicultural and diverse linguistic landscape of Brooklyn's Latina/o communities and drive home the fact that communication is not seamless even between native Spanish speakers and immigrants. Soon after, Esteban returns to the ship and begins including *güey* in his speech, something Bernardo quickly notes. He asks him about it, and Esteban replies: "I caught it from her, I guess," thus illustrating the way in which language travels and becomes adopted in new contexts (227).

Although marked by linguistic diversity, Brooklyn's Latina/o immigrant community proves to be a source of salvation for Esteban and the crew. Joaquína and her boss, the salon owner, Gonzalo, offer Esteban food, shelter, and clothing and help him to acquire a job. Esteban at first underestimates the extent of migrant solidarity and worries that Gonzalo, who fled communism in Cuba, will reject him for his participation in a leftist war. Gonzalo does not use Esteban's past against him—"We do not discriminate against nice people here"—but encourages him to revise his own narrative for the purposes of making an asylum claim (267). "It will be much easier for you to get legal status here when you tell them you're fleeing those maldito Sandinistas," the Cuban exile advises (267). This attention to difference within New York's Latina/o immigrant world evidences how characters in the novel retain political distinctions, "even while gesturing toward panethnic possibility."[23]

Joaquína suggests that the two of them attend Friday night dances at a Salvadoran restaurant where Esteban meets other Centroamericanos. "On his very first Friday night there, Esteban met a fellow Nica who worked as foreman at a chair fábrica, and who wrote down its address and the name of the nearest subway stop and told him to come by on Monday morning" (361). Through this connection Esteban is hired and is able to provide for himself and the crew. Many others from the crowd at the restaurant offer assistance to Esteban when they learn of his situation. "When they learn of Esteban's ambiguous refugee status from a phantom ship on the Brooklyn waterfront, [they] offer him a temporary place to stay, a couch or floor to sleep on until he and Joaquína find their own apartment. He always writes their names, addresses, and telephone numbers into a little pocket-size notebook Joaquína gave him for just this purpose" (362–63). For Shemak these connections reflect the only successful act of testifying undertaken by any of the crew. Bernardo, whose testimony concerning his wound would carry the most weight, is unable to offer his narrative, and the ship visitor is skeptical about his ability to bring justice based on the testimonies of the surviving crew. Only when Esteban speaks with other displaced Central Americans does "testimony seem to provide hope."[24] This list of names and numbers is what allows the majority of the crew to stay in New York. After the ship visitor tells Esteban the truth about what happened to Bernardo, Esteban realizes where he is and what he must do. He concludes that Bernardo's fate is also his own and that of those he lost in Nicaragua: "it's something that's been done to all of them . . . and it makes it also too much like what happened to la Marta and to how many compas . . . another thing he's never understood until right now" (369). Placing Bernardo's fate alongside Marta's and his own, Esteban pinpoints both capitalism and authoritarian regimes as the source of danger and death. In fact Bernardo is disappeared by Mark and Elias, an act that brings to mind *los desaparecidos*, those disappeared by military dictatorships throughout Latin America; here again Mark and Elias become interchangeable with other and earlier forms of despotic power, and the novel connects injustice throughout the hemisphere.[25] As a result Esteban understands that he must be the architect of his own liberation, and so he "calls in sick at the fábrica [factory] for the first time ever, and then he makes all his other phone calls, leafing through the little address book with fingers numbed and aching from the cold" (369–70). In the end it is not the Seafarer's Institute or the U.S. justice system that free the crew of the *Urus;* it is the enterprising work of one of the crew himself, aided by a larger community of immigrants, refugees, and exiles. When Esteban is able to place himself firmly in relation to those in his near and distant past, he attains the clarity and resolve to end the crew's existence on the *Urus* and start a new life in New York.

Transformations: Life, Loss, and Love

At the same time that the text challenges demarcations between the past and present, the here and there of war, migration, and exploitation, it also questions the separation between life and death. One recurring aspect of this in the text is the connection between sex and death. Specifically, heterosexual sex with its life-creating possibilities occurs alongside and in relation to corporeal annihilation. Sex and death are joined most prominently through Esteban's memories of his lover, Marta. Marta came into Esteban's life after her battalion suffered horrible losses at the hands of the Contras. The carnage of war brings them together. However, their time together is brief. When Marta appears in the narrative, readers have already been told that she has died. The sections that narrate Marta and Esteban's time together, we know, are merely interludes before she is killed. These interludes, the short weeks the two soldiers spent together, are filled with furtive sex as though they know how little time they have left together. The lovers futilely think about the future during their time together. The narrative describes their bodies and thoughts after making love: "Ay, Esteban, will she ever get to feel clean and smooth all over again? (Never.)" (176). The ominous "never" is death creeping into their relationship, disrupting their moments together and reflecting how Esteban's memories of Marta are steeped in sex and death.

In addition, the *Urus* is often referred to by its crew as a ghost ship, and the ship is haunted by several kinds of specters. These ghosts remind the crew and readers of the tenuous demarcation between life and death. Two characters in particular are linked to each other and to death: Bernardo and the cat he adopts and names Desastres. Desastres, also the name of the second section of the novel, appears on board the *Urus* one day. Bernardo's name for the animal, Disasters, serves as a counterpoint to the name of Mark's dog, Miracle, also the name of the shipping company under which the *Urus* is registered. Bernardo naming the cat Desastres solidifies his status as the only member of the crew with an accurate understanding of their situation. Along with his premonition that the *Urus* will sail when the Statue of Liberty walks, Bernardo is clearly and immediately able to name the futility and danger of the men's predicament.

Bernardo bonds with Desastres and even teaches the creature to sit, but one day, as suddenly as she appeared, Desastres disappears. Bernardo remains haunted by her presence, thinking of her often and even imagining that he smells her presence, marked by urine aboard the ship. "He'll feel the cat's presence, will be certain he can smell cat urine in random corners of the ship though no others will mention that they smell it too" (125). Desastres, whose disappearance leads Bernardo to consider the existence of life after death, foretells more doom for the crew and in particular for Bernardo. The burn that eventually leads to Bernardo's death is also linked to the cat. Just as he is grasping the smoking oil, preparing for José Mateo to add the rice to make the men's dinner, Bernardo "feels something brush with soft static against his calf and the soft solid thump of the cat's tail, and he turns with a breathless shout of 'Desastres!' and his heels slide out on something slippery underneath and he lands on the deck holding the pot tilted over his leg" (237). In this incident Desastres seems to call out to Bernardo to join him, and the specter of the cat leads to the existence of another haunted, lost soul for the *Urus*.

While Bernardo and Desastres haunt one another and the crew, the ship itself is a specter. According to DeGuzmán the *Urus* "becomes the site for the crossing of paths of the living and the dead." (DeGuzmán, Buenas Noches, American Culture, 173) The men mourn their dead as they are transformed into the dead, either literally as Bernardo, or figuratively as the crew are "socially dead to the world" (173). As a ghost ship, a ship of and for the unliving and unrecognized, the *Urus* calls on readers to consider the porous boundaries between life and death, the exploited and exploiter, and the past and present.

In Summary

Many of the approaches to *The Ordinary Seaman* have explored how the exceptional circumstances that the men face are not so exceptional at all. The crew join centuries of exploited, enslaved, and uncompensated laborers, connecting them with those held captive against their will in the past as well as migrants and slaves today. While the text is transnational in scope and references, the novel is also distinctly American in its approach to the Western Hemisphere and the connections between its nations. In his acknowledgments Goldman wrote that he changed the nation under whose flag the ship was registered from Liberia to Panama, a not insignificant change. Bringing Panama in explicit relationship to the ship's exploitative and criminal co-owners alludes to U.S. intervention in Panamanian history through the nineteenth and twentieth centuries from the creation of the nation to the 1989 invasion to oust President Manuel Noriega. This attention to connections between American nations makes it a "hemispheric" novel, encouraging readers to reimagine geographic and economic spaces, by placing, for example, New York in relation to Nicaragua.[26] The text's attention to Latinos and Latino-ness in particular are also what makes the work peculiarly American. Phrases such as *los proyectos* reflect the latinization of the United States and allude to the necessity of developing and employing not only new ways of thinking but also new ways of writing and speaking about the multiple peoples that have always been part of the U.S. nation.[27] As a result *The Ordinary Seaman* suggests that the United States is, and always has been, a transnational space and that transnational, and specifically trans-American, processes and peoples will continue to shape the makeup of the region.

CHAPTER 4

A View of History from the Center

The Divine Husband

In his third novel, *The Divine Husband,* Goldman continued to mine the depths of inter-American relations and exchanges but traveled into the past to do so. While *The Ordinary Seaman* ruminates on very contemporary questions of labor, commerce, and migration in an increasingly globalized world, *The Divine Husband* moves more than a century earlier, to the mid-1800s, far prior to any discussions of transnationalism or globalization. Despite the temporal distance between the two stories, common elements and ideas abound. *The Divine Husband* is very much a hemispheric or trans-American novel, narrating the lives and loves of a cast of characters who move between Cuba, Central America, and the United States. If *The Ordinary Seaman* sheds light on how militarism and capitalism have created inextricable ties between Central America and the United States in the late twentieth century, *The Divine Husband* offers a prehistory of these ties illustrating the social, political, literary, and intellectual exchanges between the regions over the last two centuries. While the Central American nation in which the novel takes place is never named, the novel includes as characters historical figures tied to Guatemala, suggesting this nation is the setting for its events. We may understand *The Divine Husband* therefore as akin to *The Long Night of White Chickens* in its privileging of the story of Guatemala specifically, a country to which the author is intimately connected. *The Long Night of White Chickens* casts light on the ways in which Guatemala, and other Latin American nations, have been marked by the United States; *The Divine Husband,* however, looks at such history from a different perspective, detailing how the United States has been shaped by Latin American peoples and nations.

The Divine Husband tells a story that spans centuries, hemispheres, and even physical realms. The text is framed by a narrator who explains that his story is the result of research he has been hired to conduct by a woman who wants to get to the root of her paternity. She wants to know if she is the descendent of her grandmother's relationship with the Cuban poet and revolutionary José Martí (1853–95). This narrative framing creates a scaffolding for the text, reminding readers that the story itself is the result of the narrator's research and writing in our present moment. However, the majority of the story takes place in the nineteenth century, where it moves between several decades, from the mid-1800s to a time fourteen years in the future and then back again. All the while, though, and in spite of the ostensible pursuit of a paternal link, the story remains focused on one woman, María de Las Nieves Moran.

The opening chapter takes place in a convent in an unnamed "capital city" during significant political upheavals. There we enter the world of Francisca ("Paquita") Aparicio and her best friend, María de las Nieves Moran, the foremother of the woman who hires the narrator. At this point, however, María and Paquita are merely children who have joined Nuestra Señora de Belén at the behest of Paquita's parents, who seek to remove her from proximity from her suitor, Justo Rufino Barrios. Both Paquita and Barrios are based on historical figures, and like the character that bears his name, Barrios (1835–85) was a military leader before going on to rule Guatemala from 1873 to 1865.[1] At the start of the novel, Barrios has not yet seized power and is instead the military commander of the province of Los Altos. Still his growing power is clear, and the Catholic Church fears his rise as he has expressed animosity toward the power of the church. Before taking control of the country, Barrios had threatened to close down all the convents, an action that was in line with his liberal, reformist ideas and that the novel suggests was also a ploy to grant him access to eleven-year-old Paquita. The young girl is portrayed as a spoiled and power-hungry schemer herself who delights in the attention she receives from Barrios and later her position as First Lady of the republic. When the narrative starts, however, Paquita's schemes are threatened by María, who asks her friend to swear to remain a virgin as long as she and then devotes herself to becoming a nun, thus assuring that Barrios will never have access to Paquita. Barrios does soon succeed in taking power and orders all the female religious communities, each with various customs, habits, and traditions, to consolidate into one. Just days prior to soldiers arriving to force the inhabitants of Nuestra Señora de Bélen from their convent, María confesses a sin to a priest and is ordered into a cell. There she is abandoned for several days until after Barrios's forces have overrun the convent and a priest returns to free her. Both Paquita and Nieves are severed from their vows by Barrios, although María has the added mistreatment she faced as a novice nun to drive her from religion.

Subsequent chapters move in time and space to grant readers access to two more periods in Paquita and María's lives: their young adulthood when they were estranged and their eventual reconciliation and comigration to New York. Approximately one-third of the narrative takes place in each of these time periods: their childhood in the convent, their young adulthood living separate lives in the capital, and their conversations while traveling by ship to New York. Following their childhood, the girls entered different worlds but remained in physical proximity to one another. After the abrupt end to her time as a novice nun, María returned to secular life and eventually sold a house that she inherited from her late father, allowing her to purchase a modest residence in the capital city. There she taught herself English and acquired a job as a translator for the British legation. Paquita remained by her husband's side throughout his rule, one that included conspiracy, murder, and torture, and death threats against her and her children. Although María continues to live in proximity to Paquita, at one point invited to a party at her former friend's house, the story remains very much María's, and readers learn about her family history, her romantic affairs (she has two children out of wedlock), her employment status and of course, her friendship with Martí.

As the Primera Dama (First Lady) of the nation, Paquita was gifted a mansion in New York by her husband, and throughout the years, and despite their emotional distance, she frequently offered María the position of governess to her children, a job that would require months with the family in their U.S. residence. Finally, years after the initial offer, and just days after Barrios's murder, María accepts and thus joins her old friend and her family en route to New York. Aboard the *Golden Rose* the two childhood friends attempt to get to know one another again and to understand the disparate choices they have made and life paths they have taken. Through their conversations we learn that the father of María's child is unnamed and that Paquita is unrepentant concerning the crimes of her late husband's regime. Here the two young women, with the help of the narrator, fill in aspects of their own young adulthoods as well as Martí's life after he left Guatemala, specifically the ten years he spent in New York. They are aided in their endeavor by files Paquita has obtained from a Pinkerton detective agent who was paid to keep tabs on the poet and revolutionary. The women's conversations are filled with wit and innuendo. When Paquita dumps a jar containing her late husband's heart into the ocean María suggests that Paquita should have "fed it to the sharks" (81). Later Paquita presses María to name the father of her child and, when María refuses, Paquita insists that one day María will have to reveal him to her daughter. María pointedly replies, "One can always invent a story. A story can certainly be a better father than a real one" (86). The idea that a story may be better than a living person is important to the novel as a large section of the narrative fictionalizes Martí, one of the great men of Latin American politics and letters.

The temporal middle of the narrative, which covers the years that María spent in the capital city prior to her decision to join Paquita and her family in moving to New York, is filled with a large cast of minor characters and long descriptions of their lives and backgrounds. These characters include a Hebrew British immigrant and entrepreneur, Don José Przypyz, his "half-Indio, half-Yankee" friend Mack Chinchilla and Chinchilla's associates, the Jewish Moroccan Nahón family. The final temporal section of the story takes place after the women emigrate and make new lives in the United States, which involves, for María, marrying Mack Chinchilla. In an epilogue the narrator reminds us of his charge and offers his own personal connections to the material, some of which parallel elements of Goldman's own life.

While the historical time period during which the novel is set is far afield from Goldman's own life, aspects of the narrative do reference his binational heritage as well as some of his personal experiences. The author is originally from Massachusetts, the state where his main characters eventually settle. In an interview he spoke about growing up in a town with a significant rubber factory, whose owner lived in Guatemala. This sparked the author's interest and brought about his desire to "invent a family with roots in the nineteenth century that unites New England [and] Guatemala."[2] Goldman also worked aspects of his childhood into the plot. While a novice nun, María develops the habit of pulling a thread of wool from her clothing and tickling her nose with it until she sneezes. A seemingly innocent action, her sneezing is nonetheless viewed as a self-indulgency and eventually earns her the punishment of time spent alone in a cell, which coincides with Barrios's closing of the convents and the abandonment of the incarcerated young nun. Goldman noted that he also made himself sneeze as a child and that in the course of researching the novel he discovered that in fact a priest had written a treatise on sneezing.[3] This integration of extensive research with his own personal experiences is characteristic of Goldman's work and reflects his expert blending of fact and fiction, something *The Divine Husband* does extensively in its portrait of José Martí.

José Martí

In her attempt to determine the paternity of María's daughter, Mathilde (the woman who years after her mother's death hires the narrator for the same reason), Paquita accuses her old friend of having been involved with her writing teacher, José Martí. Paquita promises to tell María all that she knows about Martí, from the Pinkerton detective file she has acquired, if María will reveal her daughter's father. María refuses, but subsequent sections of the novel fill in more of what transpired between the time that the convents were closed and the death of Barrios, a time that included María's friendship with Martí. Here the novel crosses back and forth between history and fiction, as it scripts María as a character into the historical period, lasting just over a year, that Martí spent in Guatemala while in exile from his native Cuba.

In the fictional world of the novel, Martí meets both young women during his (historical) stay in Central America and through his profession as a composition teacher in the Academia de Niñas de Centroámerica (Central American School for Girls). He teaches an evening writing class taken by María as well as other important members of Guatemalan society, including María García Granados (1860–78), the daughter of the ex-president of the republic. García Granados is another historical figure and has long been speculated to be the object of one of Martí's most beloved poems, Verso IX or "La Niña de Guatemala" (the Guatemalan girl). Read autobiographically, and with the speaker as Martí and the girl as García Granados, the poem aligns with several aspects of Martí's life during the time he spent in Guatemala, also detailed in the novel. When Martí came to Guatemala, he left a fiancée, Carmen Zayas, in Mexico City. According to Goldman's narrator, Martí moved to Central America partly to prove to his wealthy father-in-law-to-be that he could support himself and his future wife (*The Divine Husband,* 249). The narrator writes that during their time apart, Martí befriended García Granados and that "whatever actually occurred between Martí and [she], there is plenty of evidence to conclude that it was one of the most important emotional episodes of his life" (252). Aspects of the third stanza of the poem specifically are explored in the novel. For example, the poem tells us that when the lover returned he did so "with his wife" ("Él volvió con su mujer"). The poem also speaks of a pillow given by the young woman to her lover ("Una almohadilla de amor"), discussed in the novel when García Granados gives Martí a pillow, salty with her tears, in the hopes that he will change his mind and not return to Mexico (280).

While the novel affirms the story of García Granados's relationship with Martí, the narrator also speculates about the poet's relationship with other women, telling readers of rumors, passed down for generations, that Martí's time in Central America was his "most sexually active" (249). This creates the possibility that María de las Nieves Moran was also a lover of Martí's. In a memorable scene Martí accompanies Nieves on a walk, just prior to his leaving for Mexico. The two kiss. Immediately the narrator questions him- or herself and seeks to find confirmation of the occurrence in Martí's writings. "Is that what really happened . . . between María de las Nieves and Martí? . . . In the volume of Martí's *Collected Works* . . . the reader finds [a mention of a burning kiss]" (265). The narrator goes on to dissect the language of Martí's scribbles, acceding that some of the language echoes that used to describe *la niña*, suggesting that this kiss was shared with that same person, García Granados. And yet details differ, a kiss on the lips or cheek as opposed to the brow, suggesting it was shared with a different woman (265). While the narrator evaluates different possibilities, his musings are taken up by other characters, including Paquita, who says that the kiss was reported to her by someone who witnessed it. This blending of fact and fiction is standard in the novel, where the historical, but fictionalized figures of García Granados and Martí are placed alongside María and other invented people. The effect is to situate fictional and historical figures, story and history, on an equal plane and to suggest that the stories we know about Martí and his love affairs are as factual, no more, no less, than the stories we may know about any other character.

In terms of the ostensible driving force behind the narrative, the search for confirmation that María had a child with Martí, the novel presents a unique —or ludicrous, or clever (depending on your perspective)—resolution. We come to find out that Martí was not Mathilde's father. That distinction went to a young man whom María was hired to teach to read. The man, who is introduced to María as "His Majesty, William Charles Frederick, King of Mosquitia," is a Central American youth who became involved with the British legation in a scheme to claim power over the Mosquitia territory in Nicaragua (375). In the course of their relationship, María learns the truth: "William" has no claim to any throne. After a brief affair "William" disappears from the city without notice to fulfill his mission, taking María's servant, María Chon, with him and leaving the protagonist pregnant. María, however, does assert Martí's role in the conception of her second child, Carlos. As mentioned earlier, while they are traveling together to New York, Paquita gives to María the Pinkerton detective agency report on Martí, assembled during his time in New York. Throughout their journey (and the span of the novel), María reads from the report, allowing her and readers to put together the pieces of Martí's lives from multiple sources, including spies hired to befriend him. Late one night María reads the account of one of the agents, Miss Paral, who records her attempt to seduce Martí to gain more information. Tipsy from drinking brandy, María wanders up to the deck of the ship and fantasizes about Miss Paral and Martí, imagining herself in the spy's place. On the deck she runs into a young handsome sailor who has caught her eye for several days and who reminds her of her former lover and Mathilde's father, "William." María has sex with the young sailor, while fantasizing about Martí and "William." She imagines the sailor to be the ghost of her former lover, "a beautiful adolescent ghost for a lonely young woman who has drunk too much brandy and read too deeply" (431). Thus is María's second child, Carlos López, conceived.

When Mathilde tells the narrator this story, the narrator of course refuses to believe it. The narrator points out that, given the timing of Carlos's birth and the fact that it occurred after María and Martí were *both* living in New York, Martí could be the boy's father. However, the text offers another perspective, one that harkens back to María's time as a novice nun. During her time in the convent, she was extremely interested in Sor María de Agreda, a seventeenth-century Spanish nun. Sor María was a mystic who claimed the ability to bilocate and specifically reported that she was able to visit indigenous tribes in what is now New Mexico, without ever leaving Spain. Her presence in New Mexico was confirmed by the local people when they were visited by a priest. Goldman's María, then, seems to have simply expanded on Sor María's experience by *tri*locating, although her corporeal feat involved a perhaps less holy mission.

Within the text María's claim to trilocation continues the book's references to elements of magical realism and also contributes to coherency within the expansive narrative. This mystical experience is discussed in the novel's last chapter but harkens back to its first, providing some narrative closure by integrating María's experiences as a novice nun into her life's trajectory. At the same time María's claim that Martí is responsible for one-third of her son's paternity frustrates those, characters and readers alike, who wish to understand the *true* relationship between the two. Here Goldman pushes against narrative expectations. Throughout the entire text, recall is premised around unlocking the mystery behind María and Martí's relationship. By the end of the narrative, readers are left with more questions than answers. But a few things remain consistent. One, fathers remain unnamed. María may know the "King of Mosquitia's" real name but she never reveals it, nor does she ever name the young sailor on board the *Golden Rose*. Only Martí is named, and he is given credit for, at best, one-third of the paternity of María's two children. The "divine husband" to whom the novel's title refers remains unknowable and unnamed. Two, the narrative remains focused on women's agency, their choices and their voices. Despite the search for paternity, the narrative is possible only because of matrilineal connections, including the stories that María told Mathilde, who refuses to question her mother's version of events. Moreover, the story that multiple men were involved in Carlos's conception removes power and attention from one, singular male, again opposing narratives with such narrow, patriarchal foci. The story of María's trilocation coincides with the structure of the novel overall as, in the service of exploring the story of only one man, Martí, readers are instead told the story of a wide range of figures and characters.

Critical and Popular Reception

Critics and interviewers found in this text a rich amount of material to mine considering Latin American history and Goldman's own binational background. Some critics, such as Adam Mars-Jones of the *Guardian,* faulted the text for its length and depth, suggesting that Goldman was "distracted by detail."[4] Such a critique echoes one leveraged against Goldman's first novel in which one reviewer found the narrative too meandering. Such a perspective is not wholly surprising, given that the text is nearly five hundred pages long. However, Mars-Jones's reading is contested by Claire Messud, who wrote that despite "its considerable length . . . no paragraph is extraneous."[5] Mars-Jones also faulted Goldman for spending too little time exploring María and Paquita's complicity with the crimes of Barrios's regime and declared that Goldman "would like to think that the figure of José Martí . . . is at the heart of *The Divine Husband.*"[6] These criticisms, however, evidence a misreading of the novel on the part of the critic. Goldman spent so little time on María and Paquita's discussion of political affairs for the same reason that Martí is not really "the heart" of the story (something the author surely knows). Great men such as Barrios and Martí are already well remembered by history and literature, and devoting more time to exploring their lives and motives does not challenge dominant historical narratives. Rather, by using Martí (and to a lesser extent, Barrios) as a way of entering into a narrative that then devotes most of its time to a fictional, female character, Goldman in fact presented a challenge to these dominant narratives. Readers are drawn into a complex story that centers around the lives of people about whom little is known. A productive result of Goldman's framing would be readers questioning the narratives that are so often foregrounded as opposed to those that are not; Mars-Jones's reading evidences his refusal to engage in such a questioning.

While misreading the role of Martí in the text, Mars-Jones did at least recognize that he is not the focal point of the narrative. A later review in the same paper, by Maya Jaggi, manages to discuss the novel without ever mentioning any character besides Martí. While Martí is an important character he is by no means the most important one. The novel unabashedly focuses on the fictional María and talks of Martí's life only insomuch as it intersects with and impacts hers. Indeed, Martí himself only appears in the narrative after almost one hundred pages of text. And when he does appear, he does so himself as an object of speculation, not even a subject in his own right. Goldman wrote: "Rumors that José Martí left behind at least one illegitimate child during his year in Central America have always centered on Poem IX of *Versos Sencillos*." (Goldman, Divine Husband, 98) As I have pointed out elsewhere, such a framing makes the rumors, not Martí, the subject and introduces him only via his effects on other characters. This perspective emphasizes how much this historical figure was "formed through discourse, including rumors and speculations" and affirms the novel's focus on the interplay between story and history.[7]

Mars-Jones's contention that Goldman's narrative gets bogged down in the details is a comment on the extensive research Goldman did on life in nineteenth-century Guatemala. Concerning these details the author explained that he was striving for a particular "aesthetic" to reflect "the way the imagination uses the past to create a synthetic fictional reality."[8] Moreover he conducted so much research over such a long period of time (he started the book before he started *The Ordinary Seaman*) that he developed a deep learning of the time period. The result was that when he began writing he did not need to consult his own books; what he had learned was now "a part of his own memory."[9] Goldman's research, which involved days spent reading Guatemala City newspapers in library archives, took a toll on his health. He explained that from "breathing in century-old dust" he got mold in his lungs and developed asthma, but "it finally went away when [he] moved to Mexico City," when the notoriously polluted capital of Mexico "scoured whatever it was out of [his] lungs."[10] Goldman also credited Mexico City with providing a suitable work environment in which to conceive and write the novel. He explained that he "dreamed the entire first chapter" of the novel after a night of drinking that culminated in "48 hours with a hallucination-filled dysentric fever."[11] This pattern continued for several days as he would dream a chapter, wake up and describe it, and return to sleep. This process accounts for the dreamlike quality of aspects of the novel, which include characters' extended descent into imaginary realms as well as Goldman's own affinity for his adopted hometown of Mexico City.

The roundabout way of telling of Martí's life challenges narratives that focus only on "great men" while the geographic travels challenge U.S.-centric and Eurocentric versions of history. Here Jaggi was correct in acknowledging how the work seeks to reframe U.S. and Latin American literatures. She pointed out that *The Divine Husband* is not a "Latin American novel written in English" but rather one that expands our understanding of the American novel to include the entire hemisphere.[12] Lee Siegel of the *New York Times* also suggested that Martí's character has an interesting way of uniting the hemisphere, and he appreciated Goldman's perhaps irreverence for historical figures when he described the narrative as one that is about the poet's "screwing and impregnating his way through the two Americas."[13]

While the novel was largely reviewed and discussed extensively in interviews with Goldman, it has received considerably less scholarly attention. One book chapter and two scholarly articles largely focus on questions of transnationalism and heterogeneity in the book. My book chapter "Judaism, Sexuality, and the Nation in Francisco Goldman's *The Divine Husband*" mines the depths of some of the text's minor characters to explore the perspective on Jewish figures. Ana Patricia Rodríguez's Spanish-language article "Genealogías Transnacionales Centroamericanas: De Máximo Soto Hall a Francisco Goldman" situates Goldman and his work within a wider nexus of transnational Central American literature. She explained that the work, which she called "una novela histórica totalizadora" (a totalizing historical novel), reflects Goldman's participation in a "circuito comunicativo transnacional" (transnational communicative circuit) that connects Guatemala to New York.[14] My article "*The Divine Husband* and the Creation of a Transamerican Subject" similarly explores the hemispheric orientation of the novel, arguing that the character of María de las Nieves calls on us readers to reorient ourselves away from the great male historical figures to appreciate the lesser-known, overlooked actors in the Americas. These scholarly works concur in their assessment that Goldman's book presents a narrative rescripting of history and literature, one that places Central America (specifically Guatemala) at its center while stressing the hemispheric connections that span centuries. While the novel's complexity merits further scholarly attention, this existing research encourages us to understand the text as American, in the most expansive sense. To that end three issues that are presented in a uniquely hemispheric context warrant exploration: female agency, technological ingenuity, and racial heterogeneity.

A Lineage of Female Agency

Given the title of the novel, the narrative reflects a stark absence of important male figures. In addition, those men that are notable because of their historical resonance and political and social accomplishments are often lightly ridiculed in the text. Barrios seldom speaks himself but is rather spoken of by other characters who fear both his power and brashness. While Martí is a significant figure, he serves more of a supporting role to characters such as María. The importance of female figures and the actions they take is portrayed on the very first page of the text when the narrator speaks of María and Paquita's vow in the convent. We are told that "the upholding or breaking of that vow between two thirteen-year-old convent schoolgirls would not only influence the history of that small Central American Republic but also alter the personal lives of some of our American hemisphere's most illustrious men of politics, literature, and industry" (3). Here the agency of young girls is notable as they are endowed with the power to influence the social and political history of an entire hemisphere! Moreover, unlike Helen of Troy, whose "face launched a thousand ships," María takes an active role in this historical drama. The vow into which she enlists Paquita was her idea and illustrates her taking control of her own, as well as her friend's, body.

María's desire for agency and the importance of female relationships in her life is apparent throughout her childhood, both in her family and in her interests as a novice nun. Readers are told that María was "discovered" by Juan Aparicio, Paquita's father, who journeyed into the jungle to find the Moran family after hearing that "far away in the mountains two women and a little girl were living on their own deep in the forest" (17). Juan is apparently so struck by this rumor that he decides to investigate its veracity, whereupon he finds María, her mother, Sarita Coyoy, and their servant, Lucy Turner. Though the three were scratching out a living, they were surviving and doing so with some particularly masculine habits, such as smoking cigars. Later in life María continues a female-focused existence when she lives in the capital with her servant, María Chon, and a boarder, Amada Gomez. There, too, she challenges gender norms of proper female behavior by "sitting alone" with male merchants and eating spicy foods which risked "[heating] the body and [awakening] lust" (105).

María's interests in the convent also place her within a female-dominated space. As mentioned previously during her apprenticeship she develops an interest in the seventeenth-century mystic Sor María de Agreda. In addition to her claims to bilocation, Agreda is known as the author of a text dictated by the Virgin Mary. As a novice nun María reads and frequently references Agreda's six-volume work *The Mystical City,* which is a biography of the Virgin Mary full of revelations about earthly and heavenly life. The young nun relates to the historical figure on the basis of their extraordinary experiences at such a young age. Contemplating Sor María de Agreda, María thinks: when her "mystical travels began . . . she was just an adolescent novice, like I am now" (41). This again affirms the power and long-lasting significance of not only women, but young women. María's interest in Agreda's work places her in a lineage of female-to-female storytelling that readers are also brought into. María learns from Agreda just as Agreda learned from the Virgin Mary. María passes down her knowledge and her beliefs to her friend Paquita and to her daughter, Mathilde. The very existence of the novel, which comes about following investigations into María's life, affirms the significance of these young women's lives. Although the novel is ostensibly about Martí, the narrative is clearly interested in the poet only insofar as he was involved with María. In fact, the narrator even tells us that he spent "years" tracking down relics from María's life. Thus the very production of the book reflects how we readers are also brought into this matrilineal narrative.

American Ingenuity: Progress and Modernity

One important theme, mentioned at the outset and continually brought up in various ways throughout the text, is that of progress and modernity. Recall that María and Paquita's existence in the convent is threatened by Barrios, who in the name of reform sought to disempower the Catholic Church. The church continues to be set against forces of secularism, which also declare themselves the advent of progress and modernity. As Barrios's power grows, he directly supplants the church: a Franciscan church becomes a telegraph office, an empty monastery becomes a military academy, and a Dominicans' cloister houses the Bureau of Liquor and Tobacco. The church stands opposed to the forces of change, which come in the form of military power, technological advances, and changing morals. Lest the church be allowed to occupy a position of moral purity, however, the text makes sure to point out the hypocrisy and ethical compromises engaged in, in the name of Catholicism. During this time of intense change, the narrator tells us, a law was passed "prohibiting clergy from naming their illegitimate heirs to any church property" (29). The necessity of such a law, of course, indicates that the practice was common and drives home the point that the battle between the church and Barrios was not so much about religion as it was about power over the country.

While Barrios and his government are linked to forces of progress, however violently they may take root, several other characters introduce technological advances to the narrative. The growing uses for rubber are linked to several characters, including María, Mack Chinchilla, and José Przypyz. When Juan Aparicio, Paquita's father, tells of first finding María and her family in the jungle, he notes that the young girl had a unique toy, a "strangely buoyant, elongated, yet gelatinous object" formed into the shape of a creature and painted (17). The "idol," as Aparicio refers to it, was fashioned out of the intestines of an animal and then twisted and tied together to resemble an animal (18). María's toy, contemporary readers will recognize, is a primitive version of a balloon animal. The use of animal intestines to create a toy shows up several other times in the text, always in relation to indigenous characters, including María Chon and the Indian rebels Mack fights alongside in the War of the Caves. This original toy evolves toward the end of the novel into its modern variant, the balloon animal made out of thinly stretched rubber, inflated with air and twisted into shapes. We are told that after they have all migrated and reunited in the United States, Mack, María, and Don José together worked to fashion the toy and unveiled their "rubber globes" at the Paris International Exhibition of 1896.

By mentioning balloon animals throughout the novel, Goldman wove a humorous subplot into his work and offered continuity to the text. The multiple mentions of the toys contribute to the self-referentiality that marks so many of his works. The balloon animals also broach two other aspects of the text, an attention to indigeneity and a questioning of historical narratives. As mentioned the balloon animals are linked to indigenous characters; their inventor is Pakal Chon, María Chon's father, who lives with the Moran family in the jungle. When Chon's invention ends up evolving into a toy premiered at the World's Fair, and an object contemporary readers will recognize, the novel suggests the significant contributions of indigenous peoples. In addition, the novel offers an origin story for these pervasive toys, purporting to tell readers their history and lineage. This in turn suggests that even the most overlooked objects (and people) have a history that bears knowing, while also calling on readers to question what other histories and narratives we may be overlooking.

The balloon animals belie the text's interest in rubber, or caucho or India rubber, as characters refer to it. These materials are most consistently discussed in relation to Don José, the umbrella salesman who works with the material to create weatherproof coats and boots. Don José is an inventor who is constantly experimenting with different kinds of weatherproof products; he works on making coats rainproof and at one point creates a special pair of boots for María. Don José's experiments also lead to a more intimate product, a condom. As with the discussion of the balloon animal, the discussion of India rubber products and specifically condoms is woven throughout the text. The first time the latter is mentioned is during an outing with the other members of the convent when María is still a novice nun. She notices a group of men gathered around Don José's shop window. Years later she befriends the shopkeeper and asks him what was displayed in his window that caused so much attention that afternoon. The shopkeeper cannot bring himself to admit the truth and instead tells her it must have been a doll that he created in his spare time, fashioned from the spokes of an umbrella and with broom straw for hair. This invention is linked to a socially marginalized person, this time an immigrant and a Jew, as opposed to an indigenous man.

In keeping with the attention paid to minor characters, the novel suggests that forces of progress have a particular benefit for those that have been marginalized and forgotten. Barrios's reign inaugurates new freedoms for women, whom we are told may now live on their own in the city. The changes that Barrios brings also function as a way of writing his small, often overlooked, country into history. The appreciation for new inventions offers an opportunity for new historical actors to enter the scene, challenging the succession of power as it has been consolidated and passed on among the rich. The first time he meets María, Mack tries to engage her in a conversation about cochineal dye (also called carmine), a red dye made from the cochineal insect that was commonly used to color fabrics in Central America in the sixteenth century. According to Mack the "brilliant scarlet" of Napoleon's forces' uniforms at the Battle of Waterloo owed their color to cochineal. "So do our small, weak countries participate in the great historical events of even the most powerful nations," Mack concludes (95). Mack's statement encapsulates the underlying essence of the text, which, much like Mack's minidiatribe on insect dye, seeks to explore the contributions of the underlooked to better-known historical events and processes.

In Mack's story appreciating particular techniques allows one to appreciate the contributions of overlooked nations. At the same time the novel also suggests that technological inventions themselves allow for new actors to participate in history. Within the narrative several characters, including Mack, María, and Martí, frequent a reading room kiosk in the Parque de la Concordia. There they read newspapers from around the world and converse with one another. Perhaps reflecting Goldman's own experience as a journalist, newspapers and the information they contain become a sign of an increasingly connected and self-aware global populace. Moreover, the circulation of newspapers across borders is linked to another form of progress, steamships that carry people and goods long distances. The narrator tells us that steamships that call at ports "all over the world" bring "foreign newspapers" to the reading room (105). Here steamships allow for the greater circulation of news, and this growth in awareness in turn allows for a greater diversity of peoples to participate in the exchange of ideas. This movement engenders the growth of a self-aware, global citizenry. According to Mack: "the newspaper makes us all citizens of the country called progress" (173). Advancements in transportation allow for the greater circulation of ideas and create the possibility for new actors to participate in the global public sphere.

The preoccupation with change and advancement continues throughout the text, following the characters Mack, María, and Don José after they immigrate to the United States. Here again the novel suggests that progress allows not only new ideas and inventions to circulate but also new peoples, as these three immigrant characters make a profound mark on their adopted countries. Once in the United States, the three go into business, striving to perfect Don José's techniques working with India rubber and monetizing its uses. Mack eventually founds the Cody Rubber Factory in Wagnum, Massachusetts, a business whose legacy the narrator is able to speak of eloquently several generations later. As I explained in my article "*The Divine Husband* and the Creation of a Transamericana Subject," the last section of the novel explores the influence that the Chinchilla-Moran family had in Wagnum, listing a "Chinchilla Road" and a "Chinchilla sports complex" in the town of the narrator's birth. The fact that the characters settle in Massachusetts, also the state of Goldman's birth, is significant: "In placing Chinchilla's factory in Massachusetts, Goldman presents an alternative version of the 'discovery' and 'founding' of the United States, proposing the story of a *mestiza/o* immigrant and wanderer in place of the story of the Mayflower and the Pilgrims."[15] In its attention to the ingenuity of characters, *The Divine Husband* allows stories of progress to be linked to historical invention, reinforcing the importance and lasting impact that diverse peoples have had on the American hemisphere.

Américan Heterogeneity

As is clear by now, *The Divine Husband* includes a large number of characters who reflect a wide variety of national, ethnic, and religious backgrounds. Very few of the text's characters live out the totality of their lives in one nation. Instead the novel focuses on people who move between and among nations: Paquita and María both immigrate from their Central American nation to New York; Martí moves from Cuba to Mexico to Central America to New York and back to Cuba; Mack immigrates from New York to Central America and back to New York; the Nahón brothers immigrate from Morocco to Central America and eventually scatter across the Americas and Africa. Nearly all the minor characters are also immigrants: María's beloved sister in the cloister, Sor Gertrudis, is an Irish Catholic woman from Yonkers, New York, often referred to (incorrectly) as La Monjita Inglesa (the English Nun). And Don José's fellow merchant and businessman is J. J. Jump, a photographer and Yankee. That so many of these characters are immigrants *to* Central America is notable. North American readers are likely much more familiar with a history of migration that moves from South to North, portraying in particular the United States as a destination for Latin American immigrants. What is much less considered or written about, however, are other migratory patterns, including North American migration southward and European migration to Latin America. Both forms of migration are omnipresent within the text. The effect is to resoundingly detail *Américano* heterogeneity in all its complexity. Not only is the United States a nation heavily influenced by immigrants and the descendants of immigrants, but the nations from which these immigrants come are themselves products of immigration. The great attention paid to diverse migrants in this historical text suggests the importance of migrants throughout history and drives home the heterogeneity of the Western Hemisphere.

While the number of migrants in the text paints a portrait of ethnic diversity, two groups of people receive particular attention, Jewish immigrants and indigenous peoples. The major Jewish characters are Don José, described as a "Polish-English-Hebrew immigrant from Manchester," England, and the Nahón brothers, immigrants from Tangier, by way of Fez, Morocco (134, 144). My essay "Judaism, Sexuality and the Nation in Francisco Goldman's *The Divine Husband*" explores in depth the relationship between Jewish characters and heterosexuality. There I argued that the novel consistently links male Jewish characters with heterosexual reproduction, as seen through the Nahón brothers' investment in "producing" a male heir and Don José's invention of condoms. Their actions are rooted in heteronormative ideas and male privilege, bolstering heterosexist ideas and institutions, namely, male sexual privilege and marriage.[16] As I have pointed out elsewhere, Don José's condoms are marketed specifically to men and advertised to appeal to male desire for protection. Don José's sign reads: "Protect yourself and your wife. You may grow old and weak before she does, and upon whose gratitude and mercy shall you depend then."[17] The product is designed to allow men the freedom and protection to operate outside the bounds of marriage; meanwhile "women are *cared* for only so that they may continue to *care* for their male spouses."[18] Similarly the Nahón brothers' desire to produce a male heir is rooted in their desire to pass down their business to a legitimate offspring, fusing patriarchy with capitalism and patrilinearity.[19] However, these characters are never themselves able to fully participate in, or benefit from, these privileges and institutions. The Nahón brothers' plans go tragically awry with Salomón's murder, and Don José, after leaving behind a wife and son in England, never remarries. I elsewhere considered these "unsuccessful" unions in relationship to the consolidation of national power under Barrios. Discussing as well the relationship between sexual and national reproduction, mainly Doris Sommer's idea that heterosexual unions in nineteenth century Latin American fiction reflect the desire for an independent, unified nation, I suggested there that these Jewish characters "develop alongside, yet distinctly outside," the liberal nation-state run by Barrios.[20] There I concluded that these complex Jewish characters contribute to the novel's attention to issues of belonging and nonbelonging as well as the story's emphasis on nonnormative families, transnationalism, and migration.

In addition to frequent references to "Hebrew" characters such as the Nahón brothers and Don José Pryzpyz, the text often mentions indigenous peoples. One of the ways that indigeneity remains at the forefront of the text is via two of its main characters who are partially indigenous, Mack Chinchilla and María de las Nieves. The specificities of Mack's "india" mother's heritage are not given, but readers know that María is from Amatitlán and is fluent in the Mam language. While the frequent references to their status as *indios* may be a way of conveying the extent to which such characters are treated by their contemporaries, sometimes the references seem to go overboard. At one point Mack takes María to the opera, and while he is admiring her, readers are told that he noticed her "curving, dusky nape" and "broad, Indian-shaped skull" (319). This passage might be a reference to the racist "science" of phrenology, which suggested that "inferior races" of people could be determined by the shape and size of their skulls. However, coming from the mind of a "half-Indio" character himself the reference to María's skull seems startling and superfluous.

At other points the mention of indigeneity is accompanied by both interest and ridicule. At one point María must inform Martí that a story he has been told, about a French-speaking Indian Jefe (chief) in Sacatepéquez, is simply a joke being played on him by Paquita and her ilk. While Martí is the intended butt of this joke, the joke nevertheless is also predicated on the preposterousness of an educated indigenous leader. Similarly, in a later section of the novel, Mack is recalling his role in an indigenous-led uprising, the War of the Caves. After making contact with a British agent, Mack is received by the indigenous leader, Juan Diego Paclom, as "Don Mister Lord Englishman Jefe" (330). Here the syntactically ridiculous string of titles and its mixing of Spanish and English terms portrays Paclom as a buffoon-like character, so awed by the status and power of nonindigenous people that he heaps additional (and inaccurate) honorifics on them. Of course much of the novel pokes fun at fictionalized events and people, often through over-the-top descriptions that strip away at the reverence with which even historical people are often held. Martí's hair is memorably once described as full of curls "swaying atop his head like innumerable just awakening cats" (215). Nevertheless, when indigenous peoples are the subject of such hyperbole and jokes, the text risks reproducing the same hierarchies of race, language, and nation that it seeks to expose.

In Summary

While for U.S.-based readers *The Divine Husband* may at first appear to bring Guatemalan history into proximity with U.S. history, closer inspection reveals that the work in fact challenges such a U.S.-centric perspective; instead the novel brings U.S. history in relation to the histories of other Latin American nations, suggesting that we U.S.-based readers reorient ourselves in relation to our southern neighbors. While many recognize the influence the United States has had on Latin America, a point that comes across clearly in *The Long Night of White Chickens* and *The Ordinary Seaman, The Divine Husband* calls on us to also recognize the influence that Latin America has had on the United States. Readers are encouraged to see flows of people, ideas, and culture from South to North, granting power and agency to Latin American peoples while stressing the interconnections between American nations.

CHAPTER 5

Confronting the Legacy of Violence in *The Art of Political Murder*

Three years following the publication of *The Divine Husband,* Goldman published his first nonfiction book. *The Art of Political Murder: Who Killed the Bishop?* (2007) is a captivating, heartbreaking, and complex analysis of the 1998 murder of Bishop Juan Gerardi Conedera of Guatemala. The text is steeped in the themes of all of Goldman's books—civil war, political violence, impunity, international connections—and, like most of his work, focuses on Central America. While *The Art of Political Murder: Who Killed the Bishop?* is a work of long-form journalism, and is overtly political in its subject matter and perspective, the text might also be understood as deeply personal. The parish that Gerardi oversaw, San Sebastián, was the same one where Goldman's mother worshipped as a child and where he himself was baptized.[1] Throughout Goldman's investigation we search with him to understand the violence and corruption that continues to plague Guatemala, to come to grips with the sources and logic behind state-backed terror, and to appreciate the extent to which events seemingly confined to Guatemala in fact have precedent and reverberations throughout the hemisphere.

The book began "as a sort of assignment" for the *New Yorker* when an editor agreed to take the piece "on spec" (66). This meant that Goldman would pay his own expenses in Guatemala but would be reimbursed if the magazine published his article. In July 1998, several months after the bishop was killed on April 26, Goldman flew to Guatemala City to begin his work. In March 1999 he published "Murder Comes for the Bishop" in the magazine. The article explains that Gerardi was well known and intelligent and possessed a "nearly clairvoyant understanding of Guatemala's tangled, extremist, and nasty politics, which made him the most trusted advisor on such matters to Archbishop Próspero Penados del Barrio."[2] The bishop was the founder and director of the Archbishop's Office of Human Rights, known by its Spanish acronym as ODHA (Oficina de Derechos Humanos Arzobispado). Under Gerardi's leadership the ODHA had released a groundbreaking report detailing state-backed crimes committed during Guatemala's more than three-decade-long civil war. This report, published in a single volume in English titled *Guatemala: Never Again!*, is known by its Spanish acronym as the REMHI (Recuperación de la Memoria Histórica). The peace accords were signed in 1996, and ODHA released its report in 1998. Two days after the release of the report, which for the first time named specific perpetrators, the bishop was murdered. Goldman's *New Yorker* piece, like the book which came after, focuses on the investigation that followed Gerardi's assassination. The article introduces the principal players in the investigation: lawyers representing ODHA, a group of investigators assembled by ODHA (on the assumption that the state prosecutor's office could not or would not pursue all leads), two state's prosecutors (the first resigned by the end of 1998), and Gerardi's colleague Father Mario Orantes. Goldman explored two theories behind Gerardi's death: one involving a gay tryst and another the trafficking in church valuables by a local gang. He also pointed out that despite these theories, both of which implicate Orantes, people in Guatemala believe the army was behind Gerardi's murder. He discussed a taxi driver who reported seeing a car with a four-digit license plate, an indication that a vehicle belongs to the military, and an anonymous tip implicating two army officers, Colonel Byron Disraeli Lima Estrada and his son, Captain Byron Lima Oliva. The article includes enough information about corruption in the Guatemalan government and Catholic Church to leave readers suspicious of any conclusions drawn by either institution. That the article covers both the arrest and eventual release of Father Mario drives home the fact that a year after his death, Gerardi's murder had not been solved.

Goldman continued to follow up on the twists and turns in the Gerardi case, some of them quite bizarre, in the years that followed. These developments are well represented in the structure of the book, which is divided into five parts: "The Murder," "The Investigation," "The Trial," "The Third Stage," and "Deciphering the Truth." The first part mimics the opening of the 1999 *New Yorker* article as it focuses on the afternoon of the last day of Gerardi's life, when the bishop enjoyed a few "whiskitos" (whiskeys) and "chistes" (jokes) at a friend's house. Later that day he dropped his sister Carmen at her home and drove to the parish house of the Church of San Sebastián in downtown Guatemala City. Two maps provided at the start of the book offer relevant visual information. One shows the location of the church, which is connected to the parish house and located in front of a park. This map also shows how the complex is located just two blocks from the Presidential Military Staff (EMP); San Sebastián and the EMP share an alleyway. The second map shows the layout of the parish house, including the garage where Gerardi's body was found. On the night he was killed, Gerardi returned home a little before 10 P.M. Gerardi usually phoned his longtime friend Juana Sanabria to tell her he was safe so when she had not heard from him, Juana began calling the parish house at 10:30 P.M. No one answered, but not wanting to disturb other members of the house, she eventually gave up. A little after midnight, Father Mario, who later reported he was awoken by light coming from the hallway, woke and went to turn out the light.[3] Noticing more lights down the corridor, he continued into the garage, where he found a body on the floor. The person's head had been bashed in with a concrete slab that lay next to the body (39). Father Mario claimed to not have recognized the body as Gerardi at first, only doing so after returning to the corpse with a flashlight. Goldman found this claim unlikely. As the author pointed out, Gerardi was a large and recognizable man. Although he was seventy-five years old, he was quite robust, weighing more than two hundred pounds.[4] He was also, Goldman pointed out, "a tall man in a country where most people are not."[5]

In the hours that followed, the garage and surrounding house quickly became filled by people. Goldman named the various organizations that were represented: the ODHA, EMP, and the United Nations Verification Mission (known by its Spanish acronym MINUGUA). Members of the parish house staff, local clergy, and state prosecutors were also present. Goldman painted a chaotic picture of this time period, which included gross negligence regarding the crime scene. Several lay people affiliated with the church mopped up the scene, including a bloody footprint found near the bishop's head, before sufficient forensic evidence could be gathered. These lay people said they were given their instructions by Father Mario, who in turn said he had asked a crime scene specialist from the Public Ministry for permission.

All the individuals and organizations mentioned in the first section appear again in the second part of the book, "The Investigation." The number of people and organizations involved grows confusing, even more so because Goldman explained that some were working for others. Goldman recounted a bizarre and defamatory request made during the bishop's autopsy that his rectum be swapped for evidence of sexual activity, a request meant to slander the bishop and blame his murder on a gay lover's quarrel. The man who requested the swab was a prosecutor for the state, who, according to a member of MINUGUA, was working for military intelligence.[6] In this section Goldman introduced several theories behind the bishop's murder. These include the "gay crime of passion," which included assault by Father Mario's German shepherd, Baloo, and one that blamed the murder on a local gang stealing items from the parish. He explained the various personalities and motivations behind these theories and detailed how they came to be discovered via anonymous tips, phone calls, and persistent investigating. This section describes the arrest of Father Mario and his eleven-year-old dog and is best read in conjunction with the "Chronology of Events" that appears at the end of the book. The section ends with the arrest of five people: Colonel Lima Estrada, his son Captain Lima Oliva, Father Mario (who is rearrested), Major Obdulio Villanueva, and the parish house cook, Margarita López (also rearrested).

The third section, "The Trial," picks up in March 2001, when Goldman returned to Guatemala for the court proceedings. By this time most of the important witnesses had made statements and then fled the country. This section ends with the convictions of the suspects named above. The military men are sentenced to thirty years in prison, Father Mario to twenty, and Margarita López is freed. The fourth section, "The Third Stage," follows the appeals process after the convictions. The events entail two sets of appeals, both of which are eventually upheld, allowing the historical convictions to stand. In 2005 an appellate court upheld the verdicts against the Limas. In this stage Goldman continued to return to Guatemala and even tracked down others related to the case who had gone into exile. Notably, and somewhat miraculously, he made contact with former prosecutor Leopoldo Zeissig, who had gone into exile in an unnamed South American city, and with key witness for the prosecution Rubén Chanax, who lived in Mexico City. The final section, "Deciphering the Truth," explains some of the aftershocks of the case and again details the almost dizzying connections between Guatemalan politicians, military men, and prisoners. In this section Goldman discussed several prison riots, which may reflect a fight for power between *maras* (gangs) and military men incarcerated, including the convicted Captain Lima. The section also mentions the brutal torture and murder of Darinel Domingo, the younger brother of one of the ODHA lawyers, Mario Domingo. Darinel, to whom the book is dedicated, can be considered a victim of both the continuation of the Guatemalan war and the search for justice.[7] This section ends with the additional upholding of previous rulings, including a 2006 ruling by the Supreme Court and a final 2007 ruling by the Constitutional Court. These rulings open up the possibility that a "Fourth Stage" of the investigation may now take place, the attempt to prosecute people higher up for their role in the murder. The book ends with a much-needed list of "Dramatis Personae" and a "Glossary of Events."

Reception

The book was well reviewed in major newspapers and literary outlets and also received appropriate acclaim from human rights organizations. The *New York Times'* Carolyn Curiel was able to distill the important information from the book, whose long list of acronyms and complicated web of people and events can be confusing. But Curiel also engaged in common tropes about the lawlessness of Latin American countries and the sources of the violence. She called Guatemala a country that is "flirting with anarchy" and glossed over the significant U.S. role in the nation by referring to decades of aid for known despots and murderers as "well-meaning U.S. military support."[8] While U.S. involvement in Guatemalan affairs may not be common knowledge, this history is well outlined in Goldman's book. Reviewers located outside of the United States, Rory Carroll of the *Guardian* and Peter Stanford of the *Independent,* illustrated a better grasp on the context of the crime. Carroll explained that the book is at times "bewildering" owing to a large cast of characters, more than a few of whom share surnames.[9] But he also recognized that much of the confusion in the investigation is due to theories "intended to shield the real killers."[10] Peter Stanford of the *Independent* took on U.S. influence most directly, writing, "It reads (and is categorised by its publishers) as 'true crime,' but in the hands of a subtle and fired-up author, this is a book that exposes the corrupt, brutal and ruthless political climate that the US has spent so many decades and so many millions of dollars maintaining in Central America."[11] These reviewers accurately captured the tragedy of the case, a tragedy that includes the fact that the architects of Gerardi's murder surely remain at large. Finally, the book was the winner of the first Washington Office on Latin America (WOLA) Duke Book Award for Human Rights in Latin America. The prize recognizes fiction and nonfiction works that pertain to human rights, justice, and democracy in Latin America in the last twenty-five years. Goldman won the prize in its inaugural year, 1998. One of the judges, Holly Ackerman, compared the book to Truman Capote's *In Cold Blood,* and another praised Goldman and the book for establishing a precedent for quality publications to be recognized by the prize in years to come.[12]

Capote's 1966 book, about the quadruple homicide of four people in Kansas in 1959, is an appropriate point of comparison for English-language, especially U.S.-based, readers. However, Goldman is in direct conversation with, indeed refutation of, another work, a Spanish-language account of Gerardi's murder of a very similar name. In 2003 two reporters, one French, one Spanish, published *Quién Mató al Obispo? Autopsía de un crímen politico* (*Who Killed the Bishop? Autopsy of a Political Crime*). The authors, Maite Rico and

Bertrand de la Grange, regarded the verdicts in the case, which implicated the Guatemalan military, with suspicion, instead seeking to place blame on the ODHA itself. According to Goldman the authors offered "a conspiracy theory of breathtaking scope . . . involving an enormous number of people and without any institutional oversight, any chain of command, or any central authority to enforce their obedience and guard their silence." (Goldman, Art of Political Murder, 267) The authors seem to display a willful ignorance of Guatemalan politics, downplaying, for example, threats that so many involved in the case received. Their book was championed by the well-known conservative Peruvian novelist and writer Mario Vargas Llosa, who reviewed it in the Spanish newspaper *El País* in 2004. It is hard to understand the motivation behind Rico, de la Grange, and Vargas Llosa's position, although Goldman suggested both financial interests and political ideology are to blame.

As a book-length investigation into the crime, *The Art of Political Murder* allows Goldman to delve deeply into the case, including its context and repercussions. The book thoroughly presents two facets of the case: the complicated, bizarre, and occasionally believable theories that surrounded the murder, and the fact that the crime and its prosecution exhibit the continuation of the civil war in whose wake it was committed. While the former may appear to be a distraction, especially given the extent to which Goldman and his sources disproved them, examining them is integral to understanding an important facet of the latter. That is, the various theories put forth about Gerardi's murder in fact reflect tactics commonly used during war: the deliberate spread of misinformation and the attempt to disguise political crimes as domestic ones.

Multiple Theories

The Art of Political Murder details two principal theories put forth in the months following Gerardi's murder. The first involves the accusation that the priests, Father Mario, Bishop Gerardi, or both of them, were involved in homosexual relationships. Perhaps Gerardi was killed by a gay lover, or perhaps he discovered Father Mario in a compromising act and was killed to keep Father Mario's secret. Father Mario is indeed a strange and suspicious figure. Goldman explained that he lived a life more comfortable than most priests: sleeping on a king-size bed imported from Europe and surrounded by luxury items including custom-made shirts, Italian shoes, and expensive watches. These items were gifts from his church godmother, Martha Jane Melville Novella, as well as his brother, Sergio. Sergio, nicknamed "el Nazi" for his authoritarian personality and admiration for the military, was also a priest and had embezzled thousands of dollars from the school he ran and had given Father Mario his beloved German dog, who cost $2,500. Father Sergio and Father Mario reflect a conservative, corrupt wing of the Catholic Church.

In addition to his lifestyle and habits, aspects of Father Mario's behavior the night of the murder drew suspicion. His account of what he did the night of the murder changed several times. He also gave discrepant reports about interacting with the *bolitos,* the group of drunks who slept outside the garage door of the parish house. He claimed that after finding the body, which he did not recognize as the bishop's, he asked the *bolitos* if they'd seen anyone. He reported that a *bolito* told him everything was fine and that Gerardi had returned home some time ago. Apparently that's when it dawned on him that the body could be Gerardi, and he returned to the garage with a flashlight. However, another *bolito,* Rubén Chanax, disputed Father Mario's account. Chanax claimed that after Mario inquired about anyone entering the garage, he [Chanax] had answered in the affirmative, noting a shirtless man had left the area. Chanax's account of this incident did not change in subsequent inquiries. Father Mario's behavior that night also drew suspicion. As stated above Father Mario asked that the crime scene be cleaned up before all the evidence could be appropriately collected. In addition, folks who gathered at the scene mentioned that in the hours after the body was discovered, "the priest emerged from the parish house, expressionless, immaculately dressed and groomed, to walk" Baloo (57).

Whatever Father Mario's involvement in the murder, these theories did not have him acting alone, and the man that Chanax reported seeing was also implicated. This man was later claimed to be seen by two of the indigents that slept in the park. According to Rubén Chanax, he was arranging his bedding a little before 10 P.M. when he heard the door to the garage open. He saw a man, medium height, muscular, and shirtless. Thinking the man was opening the door to ask the homeless in the driveway to make space for a car to exit, Chanax asked the man if a car would be exiting, to which the man replied yes. A patrol car passed, during which time the man retreated into the shadow of the garage; then he left. As Goldman explained the lack of a shirt was notable in the city, located on a mountain plateau where nights can be chilly. The other indigent, known as El Chino Iván, also had an interaction with the shirtless man. El Chino Iván testified that he saw Chanax interact with a shirtless man. He left to find some cigarettes he had misplaced, and when he returned the man, now wearing a shirt, asked him for some cigarettes. El Chino Iván sold him two and later turned over the man's payment, a two-quetzal note, to the police. After that, he reported, the man left the area.

The use of Rubén Chanax and El Chino Ivan's testimony to suggest Gerardi was murdered by a same-sex lover (either his own or perhaps Father

Mario's) reflects an attempt to blame a victim for his or her own assault and is a tactic used within and outside of Guatemala. Owing to the long-standing stigmatization of gay identity, the idea that a person was murdered by a same-sex lover serves to implicate them for their own homicide and stop the investigation. Such an accusation is not unprecedented, even within high-profile cases in Guatemala. In 1989 a U.S. nun of Mexican heritage, Dianna Ortiz, was abducted and raped in Guatemala City. In her memoir of the experience, *The Blindfold's Eyes: My Journey from Torture to Truth,* Ortiz explained that as she sought justice for her suffering, high-level Guatemalan officials disputed the very fact that she has been abducted. The minister of defense at the time, Héctor Gramajo, told investigators that she was not abducted but "had sneaked out to meet a lesbian lover." He even disputed the physical marks of torture, claiming that "the gash on [her] face resulted from a lover's spat" (Ortiz, Blindfold's Eyes, 41). The use of similar slander in Gerardi's case establishes a pattern by Guatemalan officials. Sadly, such defamation was not limited to only government members but also appeared in media. Goldman discussed the cynical way one reporter took up the charges of homosexuality. A conservative lawyer, Fernando Linares Beltranena, who wrote a regular column in a national newspaper, published what Goldman termed "a particularly strained piece of devil's advocacy." (Goldman, Art of Political Murder, 92) In it he purports to be offended that homosexuality is being viewed as a detriment, asking, "Is it defamatory to describe Bishop Gerardi as presumed homosexual?" and "How do the homosexuals feel, whether confessed or in the closet, that their lifestyle should be called an insult or a dishonor" (92). Of course Linares, like Gramajo, was not interested in the well-being or civil rights of homosexuals or justice for the victims of the crimes being discussed; his only goals were to further obscure and convolute the investigations.

The theories regarding Father Mario's involvement were consistent in asserting that he did not act alone, whether with the shirtless man or others. A corollary theory to the priest's involvement is that he was aided by his dog, Baloo. Goldman explained the contracting of a Spanish forensic anthropologist, Dr. José Manuel Reverte Coma. Based on his study of autopsy photos, Dr. Reverte Coma asserted that four puncture wounds found on Gerardi's skull could have been made by a dog. His assertions were taken seriously enough to have the bishop's body exhumed. Goldman detailed with almost macabre humor the exhumation and Reverte's bizarre antics. During the exhumation the doctor makes wrong statements left and right, noting a fracture where there is none, for example. At a press conference he stood by his theory that the marks on Gerardi were from a dog bite, despite many questions and a lack of evidence. To downplay his detractors, he referred to American experts, who were prevented by Guatemalan bureaucracy from participating as anything more than observers, as "very barbaric" (136). A year later Goldman found himself in Madrid, and he visited the professor's Museum of Anthropological Forensics, Paleopathology, and Criminology. The doctor did not recognize Goldman, who had been present at the exhumation, and claimed he was unable to discuss the Gerardi case because of its "delicacy" (179).

What is perhaps most astounding about Reverte Coma's participation is that it was sought out by the prosecution, the people tasked with finding Gerardi's killers. That so much time was spent putting forth the very unlikely involvement of Baloo by the special prosecutor, Otto Ardón, illustrates the extent to which Ardón was not interested in, or perhaps was scared of, finding the true culprits for the crime. Goldman explained that Ardón was hardly a man who would have stood up to the military. He had been previously taken off a case in which he was supposed to be prosecuting military officers accused of massacring civilians; those involved worried he was too sympathetic to the military. In this he actually shared a perspective with Dr. Reverte Coma, who had been expelled from the exhumation of a mass grave in El Mozote, El Salvador, after claiming that the dead bodies represented not dead children but rather, "adolescent guerrillas, young recruits from a race of small, malnourished men" (137). Ardón resigned from the case in December 1998. The dog bite theory and Ardón's status as a beleaguered prosecutor are well represented in the Rico and de la Grange book as well as in Vargas Llosa's review. In the latter the author claimed that Ardón was forced to resign from the case and flee into exile when he tried to develop the dog-bite theory.[13] Goldman countered that Ardón never went into exile. Vargas Llosa's assertion also calls into question who opposed Ardón's theories and investigation; he places the blame on lawyers and officials of ODHA, who were in fact coprosecutors with Ardón on the case. Their motivation for obstructing Ardón's investigation is unclear.

The comical and sad dog-bite theory (eleven-year-old Baloo was held in a veterinary clinic when his owner was arrested) is the less plausible of the disputed theories that Goldman presented in the book. Another theory was that Gerardi had discovered a smuggling ring being run out of the parish. This ring involved the stealing of church property and was masterminded by Ana Lucía Escobar, the daughter of the parish house cook. Escobar was most likely also the daughter of Monseñor Hernández and had been involved in some criminal activity, which Hernández had helped her avoid consequences for. Goldman wrote that Escobar "had been arrested for belonging to a kidnapping and crime ring, but as is customary when a young criminal has a powerful or wealthy sponsor or connection, in her case Monseñor Hernández—she and other members of the gang were released for lack of evidence." (Goldman, *Art of*

Political Murder, 156) Regarding her involvement with Gerardi's murder, the theory held that Escobar and her gang, called Valle del Sol, were stealing and selling church items—relics, artwork, icons. They were aided by Father Marío, but when Gerardi found out, he was killed. Later a former judge who claimed he was carrying out an independent investigation and chronicling his findings in a daily newspaper, Juan Carlos Solís Oliva, said he had sold this theory to the prosecutor, Otto Ardón, who was an old friend from law school (160–61).[14] Goldman called this theory a "Frankenstein monster" because it was "a good story, a seductive story, too good a story to dismiss, even too good not to wish, as a tabloid editor might, for it to be true" (163). He also explained that the judge's admission that he had fabricated the story did not stop the story from being believed because he made his confession privately, not in public. The saliency of this theory illustrates the power of the media and elites. That Judge Oliva was allowed to publish his "independent investigation" in a newspaper without question reveals the power he held, while the belief that that theory garnered reveals the power of newspapers.

Goldman spent as much time as he did detailing these debunked ideas—gay lovers, dog bites, gangs stealing from the church—to offer a counternarrative to Rico and de la Grange's book and to faithfully re-create how the case wound its way through the Guatemalan courts and media. As mentioned earlier the motivations for individuals to put forth and defend these theories is sometimes unclear. Likely there were some people seeking to air personal vendettas. For example, the theory about the Valle del Sol gang came in part through Blanca Lidia Contreras, the former sister-in-law of Monseñor Hernández. She came forward implicating Ana Lucia Escobar and her mother, Imelda Escobar, in the months following Gerardi's murder. Goldman surmised that her testimony was culled from "decades of family gossip, some of it, I would guess, true, but much probably exaggerated or invented" (158). In addition to personal, familiar grudges, those behind advancing the theories outlined above were likely seeking to protect themselves by not implicating the military; doing so would no doubt put them in danger from the powerful institution. Or perhaps they were motivated by ideological factors that really did see human rights workers and sectors of the church as nothing more than communist sympathizers who wanted to destabilize the nation. From this perspective the military were patriotic defenders of the *patria* (fatherland). In this way we must view the various theories put forth as practical and ideological continuations of the civil war, the second important aspect of the book.

Finally, in bits and pieces, as more witnesses came forward and existing ones elaborated on their testimonies, readers are able to piece together with Goldman the facts of the crime. According to Goldman the Guatemalan courts ruled correctly when they implicated three military men (Colonel Byron Disraeli Lima Estrada, his son Captain Byron Lima Oliva, and Sergeant Major Obdulia Villanueva) and Father Mario. Evidence against the military men included the license plate on a car seen by a taxi driver the night of the murder, which was traced to the Chiquimula military base. When an anonymous woman called the ODHA office instructing the prosecutors to "investigate the Limas" they looked and found that the colonel had commanded the military base in the late 1980s (84). The colonel had "an exemplary military career," and no fewer than five massacres of Mayan peasants had taken place under his command (85). Those massacres had taken place in El Quiché province, an area from which Bishop Gerardi had been forced to flee earlier in his career. The military men had several other pieces of evidence against them, mostly provided by witnesses. Lima Estrada's sister-in-law told members of the ODHA that the colonel's wife suspected he had done something terrible when she overheard a conversation between her husband and other retired officers just before the murder. In the conversation the officers exhorted Lima not to "get cold feet," and the colonel replied that they had had to do "much worse" during the war (88). The prosecution explained that the colonel had enlisted the support of his son, Captain Byron Lima.[15] The captain, who was a member of a "controversial anti-kidnapping unit" within the presidential guard, had returned to Guatemala the afternoon of the murder from Argentina. Captain Lima claimed that he had been at a bar with a friend until 11:30 the night of the murder, thereby providing an alibi, but Captain Lima's alibi was put into question by himself and others. For one, credit card receipts showed that he paid his bill at 8:22, prompting the captain to claim that he had remained in the bar several hours after paying his tab. At another point he claimed that he did not return to the EMP headquarters until midnight. In addition, another military man, Major Villagrán, testified that he saw Lima at the headquarters between 8 and 10 P.M. the night of the murder. Villagrán later recanted his own testimony.

All three military men were implicated by a member of the EMP, Jorge Aguilar Martínez, a man who worked as a waiter and janitor in the organization. Stationed at the EMP headquarters the night of the murder, just blocks from where Gerardi was murdered, Aguilar Martínez testified that he was instructed not to record which cars came and went from the headquarters. Later that night he reported seeing Captain Lima, a man he knew as Hugo, and the head of the EMP, Colonel Pozuelos, come to the headquarters. It was a weekend and Pozuelos's night off so his presence was notable. In his original reports to the ODHA team, Aguilar Martínez also reported seeing Major Villanueva the night of the murder. The ODHA team asked him to "omit" that fact since Villanueva was at the time incarcerated in the Antigua prison. As it turns out, cellmates told prosecutors that Villanueva was frequently allowed to sleep outside the confines of the prison, although none were willing to go on record. Given the power that military men were seen to wield inside and outside of prison, this assertion is plausible.

Goldman explained that key witnesses such as Aguilar Martínez and Rubén Chanax likely knew even more than they told. Chanax was singled out as a weak witness by those who disagreed with the verdict. In fact, his testimony did change over time, although according to Goldman he only elaborated on his original testimony but did not change the substance. Aguilar Martínez had been deposed prior to the trial and was in exile and not called to testify during the trial. The prosecutors did not think they needed more information, and the defense likely did not call him because he risked doing further damage. Likewise, as Chanax's testimony evolved, he began to implicate himself, thereby offering an explanation for earlier versions. He explained that he was in fact an informer for the G-2, military intelligence, and was one of a number of people, including *bolitos,* paid to keep tabs on Gerardi. Again, within the context of Guatemala, in which "even the drunks are discreet," this is not implausible (4).

Those who disparaged the verdicts called into question the prosecution's reliance on witnesses. The defense spoke of the "low level" of the witnesses for the prosecution. Goldman explained that such an accusation revealed the deep racial and class stratifications in Guatemala as these "low-level" witnesses had Indian features and surnames (261). Goldman's account also allows us to understand exactly why it took so long for Guatemala to reach the historic levels it reached with the trial. Up until that point, "no military officer had ever been convicted of a human rights crime in Guatemala" (201). One of the reasons for this was the combination of a lack of resources and violence. The lack of adequate crime labs meant cases relied heavily on witnesses. Witnesses, in turn, were targeted. They were bought to stay silent or give false testimony, or they were threatened with harm to themselves or their family members. These were not at all idle threats. At one point a member of the Valle del Sol gang, Carlos García Potanza, was asked by agents from the EMP to implicate his ex-girlfriend, Ana Lucía Escobar, in the murder, thereby deflecting attention from the military men. García Potanza refused and was soon thereafter found dead in his cell. Although the death was ruled a suicide, this was unlikely, not the least because the left-handed prisoner was killed by a bullet shot into his right temple. Goldman called this the case's "most romantic episode, appropriately fatal" (235). Nearly everyone else involved with the prosecution faced threats, including witnesses, attorneys, and judges. Mynor Melgar, the coordinator of ODHA's legal team, left the country during the investigation (he spent a year in Berkeley, California) but returned for the trial. As soon as he returned, he received threatening phone calls and once had a pistol held to his forehead as he knelt in his house, with his wife and two young sons watching. He was told this was a warning.

These threats also delayed court proceedings. One by one judges resigned from the case (out of fear), and every time a judge stepped down, the trial would be delayed while a new judge was seated. As the trial got underway, three of the four key witnesses were in exile, and the fourth was incarcerated. The special prosecutor's office was particularly targeted, and the lead prosecutor Leopoldo Zeissig received nonstop threats. His wife, a young lawyer and mother to their one-year-old child, would receive phone calls saying, "Your husband hasn't come home yet? Well, he's not coming home" (206). Later they recovered a notebook from Captain Byron Lima showing sketches of Zeissig's home and lines outlining how to enter bedrooms. During the trial Zeissig traveled with a caravan of three cars escorted by pickups full of armed police and was under twenty-four-hour surveillance. In addition, witnesses commonly testified wearing bullet-proof vests. Infuriatingly Rico and de la Grange downplayed such threats in their account, writing only that Zeissig received a phone call with a "cloying melody" playing (383). However, there is clear consensus on the use of abuse and threats on the part of the Guatemalan military, especially military intelligence. A United Nations report in 2002 noted human rights violations in the country that included "death threats and acts of intimidation, such as following vehicles, surveillance in front of the victims' homes and office, [and] anonymous and malicious telephone calls." Even the U.S. State Department's report on the country in 2001 mentioned a "parallel investigation" of the Gerardi case carried out by military intelligence that "interfered with the justice system's efforts to investigate and prosecute those responsible" (385).

Despite the successful convictions, the extent of the crime and those involved has likely not yet come to light. Aguilar Martínez had implicated military men higher up than Colonel Lima Estrada and Captain Lima Oliva. These included the head of the EMP, who reported directly to President Arzú. Aguilar Martínez reported that Arzú had been "visibly nervous" and "drinking more than usual" the day before the murder (225). The fact that the case could have involved President Arzú contributed to a lack of faith in the verdicts on the part of the larger Guatemalan society and press. By the time the verdicts came in, Arzú had been succeeded by Alfonso Portillo, who took office in 1999. Portillo was voted out of office four years later and faced corruption charges. His government "had turned out to be the most corrupt—and that is saying something—and despised administration in recent Guatemalan history" (266). Therefore, those suspicious of the verdicts or seeking to defend the military put forth the idea that the investigation and verdicts were simply part of Portillo's corrupt government. Perhaps not helping this viewpoint was the fact that Edgar Gutiérrez, who had once coordinated the REMHI, was appointed by Portillo to head his Secretariat of Strategic Analysis. This added fuel to the fire of rumors that in fact members of ODHA, specifically Gutiérrez, were behind Gerardi's murder and had blamed it on the military to displace blame from themselves. Vargas Llosa repeated such rumors in his column devoted to *Quién mató al Obispo?*, writing that ODHA's actions were "thoroughly suspicious, to say the least," and suggesting that several from the organization, including Gutiérrez, were rewarded for their lies.[16] Goldman gave no credence to these ideas; indeed the notion that someone who had devoted years to uncovering the truth during the civil war was himself guilty of murdering his coworker is far-fetched. However, the author did not offer any explanation for Gutiérrez's acceptance of the post in Portillo's government. Why would someone as knowledgeable about the criminal collaborations between the Guatemalan military and government agree to join the government? As this trial makes clear, Guatemala hardly has a history of effective reforms happening from within.

Another loose end in the account of the murder remains the shirtless man seen the night of the crime. Several people identified him as a man named "Hugo," but otherwise his identity is never discovered. Goldman even questioned whether or not he exists; might he have been a fabrication on the part of people on the military intelligence payroll to throw off the investigation? Readers of the book are left with assurance of the culpability of the people arrested but also with the assumption that neither their involvement, nor that of others, has been fully brought to light.

A Continuation of the War

Gerardi was killed just two days after the human rights office that he founded and directed (the ODHA) released its monumental chronicle of the Guatemalan civil war. *Guatemala: Nunca Más!* is a four-volume, fourteen-hundred-page report on the violence inflicted on the Guatemalan people dating from the 1960s. The report is often referred to by its Spanish acronym, REMHI (pronounced REM-hee), Recuperación de la Memoria Histórica, or Recovery of Historical Memory Project. Published in English as a single volume, the REMHI details massacres, forced disappearances, murder, rape, and torture largely perpetrated by a right-wing government against a civilian population. Reports often reference the two hundred thousand people killed during the war, but this number does not account for the total number of people who were impacted, forced to flee, or internally displaced, or the fact that a disproportionate amount of violence was meted out in the highlands of the country, where the nation's Mayan indigenous population is found. Neither does the number accurately reflect the aftereffects and later casualties of the war, such as Gerardi himself, who must be thought of as a victim of the war, despite the fact that he was murdered over two years after the signing of the peace accords in 1996. Goldman pointed out that the guerrilla forces who fought the army and government bear some responsibility for the violence, although he clarified that the army, which was not interested in any kind of negotiation, is responsible for the majority of violence. In fact, the REMHI found that 80 percent of crimes committed against civilians during the war were at the hands of the army or its affiliated paramilitary organizations; 5 percent were attributed to the guerrillas. A UN report, *Memory of Silence,* released in February 1999, found even more disproportionate numbers, asserting that the army had committed 93 percent of the two hundred thousand civilian deaths; 3 percent were attributed to the guerrillas (Goldman, Art of Political Murder, 22, 155).

Under the terms of the peace agreement, the state-backed army, who possessed considerably more financial and military power, were able to gain for themselves "sweeping amnesty" from prosecution for war crimes (5). Activists and survivors representing the left wing fought hard to have certain conditions included in the accords and remained dissatisfied with the results. For example, while the accords eventually did not allow amnesty from prosecution for "genocide, forced torture or disappearance," the crimes of "illegal detention" and "extrajudicial killings" were left out. The inclusion of "genocide" did not reflect a real victory for human rights groups, who pointed out that it was "much easier to establish that the mass killing of the inhabitants of an Indian village took place . . . than to prove such a massacre was motivated by racial or ethnic considerations."[17] As this example illustrates, considerable debate surrounded the peace process, including records meant to capture the extent of the violence. The ODHA's report was itself a response to what many saw as the insufficient report by the United Nations. Developed by the Historical Clarification Commission, the UN report was significantly more limited in scope; it refused to name perpetrators of violence or to attribute responsibility for killings.[18] However, and surprisingly, the UN report did end up accusing the Guatemalan Army of genocide.

The insufficiencies and distrust of the UN process broach larger issues with Truth and Reconciliation Commissions, which have been instituted in the wake of civil wars spanning the globe from South Africa to Peru to Rwanda. While often held up as a means through which survivors and witnesses can testify to their experiences in the service of justice, Leigh Payne explained that the processes through which commissions are conducted may reproduce, rather than challenge or reverse, structural inequality and even trauma. For example, many commissions rely on the testimonies of perpetrators of violence. Giving perpetrators the floor may yield unforeseen and dangerous results. Goldman detailed one such example, when he discussed the testimony of Colonel Lima Estrada before Guatemala's truth accords. Lima Estrada opened his jacket to reveal a recording device, telling the commission members, "I'm recording also."[19] In addition to providing the opportunity for intimidation, confessions may necessitate a response by victims and survivors whereby the latter must assert their own, "often contending, interpretations of the past."[20] Payne explained that confessions themselves are not simplistic assertions but rather require interpretation to have meaning (26–27). In addition, even when perpetrators express remorse for their actions, an undue burden may be placed on survivors who are implicitly called on to accept the proffered apology (73–74). Payne outlined some of the shortcomings of Truth and Reconciliation processes that the REMHI sought to overcome. In the REMHI emphasis is placed on specificity and multiple layers of violence so that not only are survivors' voices heard through direct narratives, but the framing of the evidence underscores the way that issues such as gender, ethnicity, language, and culture impacted who experienced violence and in what way. Gerardi's report was produced through careful and extensive training. Nearly eight hundred people were trained over a two-year period in how to collect testimonies. Care was taken to meet the needs of Guatemala's majority Mayan population, who make up at least 60 percent of the populace and many of whom speak Spanish as a second language, if at all. Over half of the interviews for the project were conducted in one of fifteen Mayan languages; the rest were in Spanish.[21]

The opening section of Goldman's book offers necessary information concerning both the REMHI and the Guatemalan civil war, which spanned nearly four decades. Goldman detailed U.S. influence, most notably the 1954 CIA-backed coup that overthrew democratically elected president Jacobo Árbenz. The coup was backed by Secretary of State John Foster Dulles and his brother, CIA director Allen Dulles, who saw in Árbenz's legalization of the Communist Party a threat to U.S. political interests as well as the interests of U.S. corporations. Foster Dulles specifically was alarmed at Árbenz's expropriation of fallow fields owned by the United Fruit Company, a company that he had once represented during his work at the New York law firm of Solomon and Cromwell. In fact Árbenz's government reimbursed the company for the land seized, basing their compensation on the value of the land that the UFC had been declaring on their taxes.[22] The coup was originally authorized under President Truman but eventually carried out under President Eisenhower. Named PBSUCCESS, the coup marked a new era of overt U.S. intervention in foreign affairs. It has the distinction of being the second time the CIA overthrew a democratically elected foreign leader. The first occurred one year prior, in 1953, when the agency toppled the Iranian president Mohammed Mossadeq. Like the Iran coup that came before it and the one that toppled Chile's Salvador Allende later, the Guatemalan coup brought to power right-wing, probusiness, and pro-U.S. politicians whose control was maintained by paramilitaries. Árbenz's defeat brought about a period of destabilization and state-backed violence that would continue for the next three decades.

Goldman pointed out some of the ironic elements of U.S. policy toward Guatemala. On the one hand the United States gave aid to the Guatemalan Army. The United States also, through the School of the Americas training camp based in Fort Benning, Georgia, trained generations of Latin American military officers.[23] These officers, officially trained in "counterinsurgency" techniques, have been found responsible for dozens of extrajudicial killings throughout the hemisphere. Among some of the most infamous graduates of the school are Benedicto Lucas García, a man independent U.S. reports found to be "responsible for some of the most brutal violations of the war."[24] Goldman, however, noted that during the 1960s, Guatemala was also part of John F. Kennedy's Alliance for Progress, which brought citizens to the United States to support moderate democratic reforms. These same U.S.-trained reformers were often murdered by U.S.-trained military men when they returned to Guatemala. In fact, Goldman reported, by 1970 *two-thirds* of those political reformers trained in the United States had been murdered. (Goldman, Art of Political Murder, 15) In a continuation of the complicated relationship between Guatemala and the United States, the U.S. embassy offered protection for witnesses during the Gerardi trial. Mario Domingo, an investigating attorney with ODHA, noted the irony of this in a conversation with Goldman. The fact that ODHA, MINUGUA, and other human rights groups rely on such support, Domingo told him, "seems ridiculous" (141).

Goldman discussed the links between the army and paramilitaries and noted that despite the war often being framed within the context of the Cold War and Soviet power, the conflict was very much about maintaining the power of a wealthy elite. The text also details the targeting of particular groups of Guatemalans, including the Mayan majority and the Catholic Church, during the war. The former were targets of violence in rural hamlets; more than six hundred Mayan villages were completely obliterated during the war. The plight of Guatemala's Maya community gained international attention when the 1982 Nobel Peace Prize was awarded to Mayan revolutionary Rigoberta Menchú. Menchú's father had been killed himself two years earlier in a fire at the Spanish embassy; the fire, started by the army, killed dozens of people seeking refuge. Menchú's *testimonio,* or life history, *My Name Is Rigoberta Menchú,* brought attention to Guatemala's Mayan population as well as the form of literature that blends autobiography with the story of political consciousness-raising.

Catholics who served rural Mayan populations were often targeted along with their parishioners. Those that were devoted to the nation's disenfranchised were often people who had been influenced by changes that took place during the Second Vatican Council as well as the meeting of Latin American bishops held in Medellín, Colombia, in 1968. Out of the latter meeting came the phrase "option for the poor" or "preferential option for the poor," which encouraged clergy to put the interests of the poor and powerless before the wealthy and powerful. Thus Catholics serving in impoverished Mayan communities often understood themselves to be doing the work of Christ while they were also perceived as a threat to the elite of the country. This targeting of Catholics occurred throughout the region during the civil wars in El Salvador and Nicaragua as well.

Goldman placed Gerardi within this context as he traced the priest's service in El Quiché province. There in the early 1980s he was forced to confront army officers and originally flee the area. In protest Gerardi closed the diocese in El Quiché. Because of threats that followed him in Guatemala and El Salvador, Gerardi was forced to go into exile in Costa Rica. There he remained, "in anguish" for three years as he watched the violence in Guatemala continue unabated; the priest who reopened the El Quiché diocese was murdered. However, once General Oscar Mejía Victores came to power in 1983, the war against the church lessened, and the new archbishop, Próspero Penados del Barrio, summoned Gerardi back from exile. As the above discussion indicates, sectors of the church, as well as anyone involved with human rights work, were considered enemies of the state by the Guatemalan military during the civil war. Gerardi's murder took place in this context as he was seen as someone who needed to be eliminated. The investigation, trial, and its aftermath indicate that these two factions, the church and human rights workers on the one hand, and the army on the other, continued to be in conflict. At the same time, not all sectors of the church were aligned with human rights work, either during the war or after.

The continued power of the military is made clear through Goldman's description of trying to piece together a case for the prosecution. As mentioned previously witnesses were killed or frightened into fleeing the country. Often people who had at one point worked for the military but were now supposedly civilians were implicated. For example, on the night before the opening arguments of the trial, two grenades were tossed into the backyard of one of the presiding judges, Yassmin Barrios. Barrios lived in a densely populated, middle-class subdivision with walled-in yards, meaning that the perpetrators needed aerial surveillance to carry out their attack, or the cooperation of neighbors, or both. Goldman noted that an investigator from MINUGUA suggested that one of Barrios's own security guards may have been involved, explaining that most security officers were former military men. The author also told readers that, one year later, the head of Barrios's security detail would be taken into custody for the extrajudicial execution of two men. This information illustrates the carryover of military protocols, technology, and culture from the period of armed conflict to the time of "peace." When people who work in security professions, including as police or bodyguards, have a military background they bring with them both their military loyalties and military tactics, which during the civil war included gross human rights violations. Judge Barrios, who was involved with prosecuting men tied to the military for Gerardi's death, could easily have been seen as an enemy of the state by her ex-military security detail. Thus we can see how the military lost neither power nor resources after the peace accords.

Certainly the men on trial, notably Colonel Lima Oliva, viewed the investigation and court proceedings as a continuation of the civil war. In an interview published in *El Periódico* in May 2001, Colonel Lima said explicitly that he was on trial because "his enemies 'wanted to win in the political sphere the military war they lost'" (240). He claimed to be framed by members of the ODHA who were aligned with a "new wave" of military men who respected human rights and civilian rule (240). The colonel also regarded Gerardi as a member of that wing of the church that opposed the military, naming "liberation theology" and those who supported it as among his enemies (241). As Goldman explained: "Everything about the Gerardi case—perhaps even the murder itself—was a continuation of the war by other means. The war wasn't over" (241). The trial specifically offered insight into the ideology of the Guatemalan military and the fact that this ideology remained after the signing of the peace accords.

Of course the ideology that viewed human rights workers, liberation theology, and priests as enemies of the state was not only held by military personnel but also supported and perpetuated by Guatemalan citizenry. Goldman described "right wing zealots" who supported the defense and attended the trial, including an elderly woman the prosecuting team nicknamed the Pink Panther (252). Dressed in flamboyant clothing, usually with pink or purple shirts, the woman sneered at the prosecution each time the defense offered what she considered a particularly clever point or rebuttal. People who perhaps shared her views were also not far from Goldman's own social circle. When his mother visited her native country during the trial, some of her elderly childhood friends repeated accusations that Gerardi was gay. He was the "*jefe*

[boss] of all homosexuals and *maras*" (street gangs), the elderly, pious, affluent women said (140). Of course right-wing supporters were met with their opponents on the left. The area where the supporters of the prosecution sat was nicknamed Woodstock by the Guatemalan press. This section was filled with "human rights activists, 'solidarity' types in sandals, progressive nuns in secular dress, and Franciscan friars in austere brown smocks" (252). In this way the polarization of the larger Guatemalan society was on display during the trial, a polarization that mimicked the divisions that existed during the armed conflict. Finally, lest U.S. readers assume that rhetoric that blames leftists for political strife occurs only in Latin America, Goldman noted that in a meeting with presidents from the Caribbean and Central America in 2005, then president George W. Bush said he was "preoccupied" by "pressure groups" aligned with the left in Central America that put "the stability of democracy at risk" (328).

Updates

The Art of Political Murder was published nine years after Gerardi's murder; now, twenty years after the crime and eleven years after the book's publication, the case continues to generate press as well as questions and heartbreak. In an interview with Daniel Peña, Goldman explained: "That book had an impact. Eight years after it was published it's still having an impact in Guatemala. I remember when I wrote it, a surprising number of people said things to me like, 'That is such an amazing story; why didn't you turn it into a novel?' *Oh yeah, all the glory for Frankie Gee, right?* Of course I never considered that. Though my name appears as the author of that book, it was written by many of us. A novel wouldn't just have been a betrayal of every person who'd told me her or his story and of all those people who trusted me to get their part in this amazing story right, it would have had no authority, and no more impact than a snowball tossed into a volcano."[25] Indeed Goldman's remarkable book must be credited with the continued attention that the Gerardi case receives in Guatemala and around the world.

Now several people indicted in Gerardi's crime have either died or been released from prison. Sergeant Major Villanueva was the first to die, killed in a prison riot in the Centro Preventivo in 2003. In July 2012 Colonel Lima Estrada, aged eighty and in failing health, was released from prison. Father Mario was released in January 2013, owing also to failing health and good behavior. Colonel Lima Estrada's son, Captain Byron Oliva, was killed in a prison riot in July 2016.[26] Prior to being killed, Oliva was a powerful figure in the prison, where he enjoyed "certain privileges."[27] His death was likely a result of internal power struggles, possibly with gangs, or *maras,* within the prison system.

While no doubt at least several others involved in some stage of Gerardi's murder remain at large, 2015 saw yet another development in the case. On September 15 President Otto Pérez Molina, having been stripped of his immunity by Congress, was arrested and charged with corruption.[28] As Goldman explained in an interview the following month, what eventually brought down Molina was evidence that the president had taken part in a corruption ring involving customs in which those involved offered importers discounted tariffs in exchange for bribes. That Pérez Molina was eventually brought down by such a common crime—Goldman called it "an extortion scheme that looks like it comes out of the Sopranos"—is incredible.[29] As Goldman explained, Pérez Molina, although never charged during the case, was implicated during the investigation. According to key witness Rubén Chanax, Pérez Molina was among the military men, including Colonel Lima Estrada, who were gathered in a bodega near the parish the night of Gerardi's murder. That Pérez Molina, who was well known to have been a member of the Kaibiles, a special forces wing of the Guatemalan Army, was involved in the case is in keeping with his involvement with extrajudicial killings. In addition the idea that Chanax was too fearful of, or perhaps too loyal to, Pérez Molina to keep his name out of his official testimony is consistent with that witness's actions.[30] For this "remarkable event," in which a man went from "president to prison" in one day, Goldman has given credit unequivocally to the Guatemalan people, who maintained pressure on the country to refuse to recuse corruption.[31]

CHAPTER 6

Love, Loss, and Literature

Say Her Name

If Goldman mined the depths of violence and impunity in Guatemala for his 2007 book, his next book necessitated a no less harrowing process, examining the origins of his own unspeakable grief and loss. His 2011 novel, *Say Her Name,* details the death of a young woman, Aura Estrada, from the perspective of her lost and bereaved spouse, Francisco Goldman. Although the names of the characters match those of Goldman and his late wife, the book is a work of fiction, albeit one based on events in the author's life.[1] Like his narrator, Goldman fell in love and married the younger, Mexican-born Estrada. The two met when she was working on her Ph.D. in Latin American literature at Columbia University. They wed in Mexico in August 2007, when Estrada was twenty-eight and Goldman forty-seven. Less than two years later, while on vacation in the beach town of Mazunte, Oaxaca, Mexico, Estrada suffered a fatal injury. A wave crushed several of her vertebrae and damaged nerves connected to breathing. She was air-lifted to Mexico City but died within twenty-four hours. The two had been married just shy of two years; Estrada was three months past her thirtieth birthday. Following her death Estrada's mother and uncle blamed Goldman for her death. They excluded him from their lives, retaining Estrada's ashes and seeking to hold Goldman criminally responsible for her death.

While all this information appears in the book, Goldman insisted, sometimes in the face of opposition, that his is a work of fiction. The author refused the term memoir, explaining that he "made things up in order to be able to tell the truth."[2] He went on to say that he "never liked the memoir form because I tend to think that memory is fictionalized anyway."[3] In a 2013 conversation with Junot Díaz and Daniel Alarcón for *Radio Ambulante,* the author suggested that the intense interest in memoir is a particularly U.S. phenomenon. He linked the phenomenon to a consumer market that, owing to popular personalities such as Oprah Winfrey, has become accustomed to the genre and a particular format that involves confession and absolution. As evidence of the national origin of this interest, he said that the genre of the book was never once mentioned by Latin American or European reviewers. He also offered another explanation for his own hesitation to employ the memoir format, explaining that for his generation, memoirs are closely related to *testimonios*.[4] A hybrid genre that tells the story of a larger community focalized through one person's experiences, and related specifically to issues of political consciousness-raising and social justice, *testimonio* for Latina/os and Latin Americans of Goldman's generation is represented by important books such as the Guatemalan Rigoberta Menchú's *Me llamo Rigoberta Menchú y así me nació la conciencia* (*My Name Is Rigoberta Menchú*) and the Nicaraguan Mario Payeras' *Los días de la selva* (*Days of the Jungle*). Despite Goldman's protests, however, discussion of the book as a memoir has persisted. A National Public Radio piece on the book calls it a "novel-cum-memoir" and then goes on to note that "the best novels about marriage acknowledge that there is something hidden, something unknowable within to all outside parties."[5] Moreover, critics, reviewers, and readers continue to find the book's relationship to the author intriguing and vexing. For one critic the interspersing of references to fictional and nonfictional authors contributes to a certain amount of "distraction" in the text.[6] For example Francisco and Aura meet at an event for the (fictional) Mexican author José Borgini and attend a dinner party that includes the (nonfictional) British Indian author Salman Rushdie. The reference to figures such as Rushdie may compel readers to try to deduce the identities of other characters mentioned. Larger questions, such as whether or not Goldman did sleep with one of Aura's best friends after her death (as the character Francisco does) led one critic to lament that "doubting the narrative's truth-value set up an annoying stumbling block and I found myself asking fruitless questions."[7] Despite this critic's annoyance, the novel received favorable reviews from major newspapers including the *Boston Globe,* the *New York Times,* and the *Guardian*. It also received international recognition in the form of the French Prix Femina étranger.

In response to readers Goldman has addressed directly some of the "facts" versus "fictions" in the memoir. He explained in an interview with *Publisher's Weekly* that unlike Francisco, he never quit his job or lived off Aura's savings. Interestingly he also based his desire to call the book a novel in his experience as a journalist and his respect for the distinctions between fiction and nonfiction. "I've never agreed with the idea of making composite characters, or moving events around in time, exaggerating, and still calling it nonfiction."[8] Here the author referenced the growth of creative nonfiction, a genre that employs elements commonly associated with fiction in the service of telling stories based in fact. The genre encompasses biography, memoir, food writing, and travel writing and has experienced a sharp increase in terms of both readers and writers in recent years.

Goldman also claimed that he had no sufficient model for this work, no novelist he could turn to who had also lost a spouse. Rather he compared himself to a character from Euripides's play *Alcestis*. In fact, he compared himself to two characters, King Admetus, who loses his wife Alcestis, and Heracles, who rescues Alcestis from Hades. He is, he explained, both the husband who "loses everything," and, through his writing, the man who brings his wife back to life.[9] Again Goldman's own perspective on the text is not uncontested. Patricia Connolly compared the author to the novelist, playwright, and memoirist Joan Didion, whose *The Year of Magical Thinking* (2005) responds to the death of her husband, John Gregory Dunne, and the illness of their daughter, Quintana. Armando Celayo agreed, comparing the book to Didion's as well as Joyce Carol Oates's *A Widow's Story*, although he concluded that the best comparison is Leonard Michael's *Sylvia*. The comparisons are apt, the critic explained, because these texts are not confined by "factual restraints" but rather "employ narrative techniques found in fiction."[10] These techniques include the careful plotting of the narrative, the re-creation of conversations according to what the author imagines Aura might have said, and the fictionalization of particular people.

While containing aspects of both memoirs and novels, the text bears resemblance to another prominent nonliterary genre, a criminal defense. The opening page reads like the presentation of the basic facts of a case; the narrator even says, "It's not as if I consider myself not guilty."[11] Moreover Goldman left until the end of the novel the account of Aura's death. He explained that he was unable to write that section until later in his own mourning. But he also suggested that leaving the details of Aura's death until the final pages allowed the narrator to present his case: "if you think of it as a criminal case, you are trying to study everything that led to the moment in question. Was it a crime or not?"[12] In fact *Say Her Name* may be seen as all these things—a memoir, a novel, and a self-defense of its author. It is also a meditation on mourning, a portrait of love and marriage, and a biography of Aura Estrada. In addition, although the book is about Francisco and Aura (the characters), the text features another prominent protagonist—the country of Mexico.

Aura

Throughout the novel Aura emerges as a vibrant, intelligent, ambitious, and anxious woman. Francisco captures his late wife's impulsive and impractical nature by describing her approach to things she loved. Early in the text he recounts how she purchased a multicolored quilt while visiting friends in upstate New York. Not only did she lie to him about the price, claiming that it cost $150 instead of $600, but Aura also fought with Francisco over bringing the quilt to Mexico. Aura's desire was completely impractical; the couple was going to Mexico only for the summer, and bringing the quilt would entail hauling an additional suitcase there and then back again in September. Francisco recounts this potentially frustrating incident with both humor and understanding. He describes how Aura fumed while he "had to bite the inside of [his] cheek to keep from laughing." (Goldman, Say Her Name, 26) He also understands that she lied about the price not only because it was so expensive but also because his wife did not want him to think of her as the "kind of woman" who would spend so much money on one item (27). The fact that he understood so well her motivations demonstrates that Francisco's love was accompanied by a deep understanding of his wife.

Aura's interest in beautiful things extended to an obsession with beauty products—creams, lotions, and so on. She was perhaps self-conscious about this obsession, leading her to jokingly, futilely, encourage her husband to consider male cosmetics, even Botox. Francisco took her pestering as jokes, a way of playfully drawing attention to their age difference. Related to that Aura joked about their physical differences constantly. One of their "routines," Francisco recounts, involved Aura exclaiming, often after just waking up in the morning: "Ay, mi amor, que feo eres. Por qué me casé contigo? . . . Oh my love, how ugly you are. Why did I marry you?" (28). Aura seemed to delight in mocking him physically. He relates how an old high school football injury left him with a knee that gave him trouble when descending steep stairs, necessitating that he takes every step with that leg first. In addition, on cold damp days, his aching knee would cause him to limp a bit. As a result, Aura would imitate his limp. "To people behind us on the sidewalk we must have looked pretty comical," Francisco suggests (333). Francisco does not seem to mind these playful insults and rather seems to appreciate Aura's frank articulation of their differences in age and appearance. He relates a conversation based in Aura's fear that "she was condemning herself to a miserable early widowhood by marrying" Francisco (237). In his self-deprecating manner, Francisco assures her he will not live longer than seventy-five, at which point Aura will be in her fifties and still beautiful and able to marry a handsome younger husband.

While these anecdotes perhaps portray Aura as playfully cruel, they nevertheless also exemplify the deep love between the two protagonists. Francisco never once doubts the depths of Aura's love for him. Rather Aura's playful ribbing seems to confirm to Francisco the great luck that he has stumbled upon, in love with a woman whom he perhaps does not deserve. This idea is supported by a picture of the author and Estrada at their wedding that often accompanies reviews of the book. In the picture Estrada is leaning forward, grasping Goldman by the hand but looking to a spot just in front of her. Goldman is more static, one hand is in Aura's and the other grasps a small tequila drink. His feet are planted firmly on the ground and he is facing the camera directly, his mouth in a wide-open laugh, eyes scrunched tight from the strength of his smile. His face seems to render incredulity as though he is trying to take a moment to consider the amazing good fortune that has brought him to this moment. This picture captures the goofy joy that author and narrator report during their short time with Aura/Estrada. For her part, and despite her taunts of having a "feo" (ugly) husband, Aura was not dissatisfied. Francisco recalls a tender moment in the spring before she died while the two were at home in Brooklyn; Aura turned to him and exclaimed: "We have everything we need to be happy. . . . Do you know how lucky we are?" (237). The luck that Francisco attributes to his happiness was in fact a feeling they both shared.

While these episodes suggest a childlike side of Aura, the book is resolute in portraying her intellectual and emotional depth. Much of this is conveyed through her own interest in psychoanalysis and her family history. As Robin Romm of the *New York Times* noted, one of the most admirable qualities of the book's portrayal of Aura is the narrator's "reverent respect for her mysterious inner life, for the complex variables that kept her partially unknowable."[13] Aura is obsessed with understanding why her father abandoned her, not only divorcing her mother but refusing to play a part in his child's life. The lack of a father marks Aura and continues to impact her into adulthood. Francisco conveys these feelings, and he himself attempts to get to know his late wife more through Aura's writings, both childhood journals and unpublished creative writing. The narrator places particular value in her writings because he has been denied access to what remains of Aura physically as her mother retains her ashes. The novel that Aura was working on suggests keys to several mysteries: Aura's feelings about her father, her relationship with her mother, and the impact of psychoanalysis. All three elements play a major role in her writing as her novel focuses on a French Mexican psychoanalyst who falls in love with a Mexican woman but many years later ends up marrying his ex-girlfriend's daughter. The characters' names echo Aura's and her mother's; the young woman is named Alicia and her mother, Julieta.[14] While Francisco notes the potential relationships between Alicia and Aura, he cannot help but try to understand his own role in the novel/family drama, suggesting that the older psychoanalyst might be him. Francisco's discussion of Aura's novel illustrates the complex interconnections between families, narratives, and psychology that the larger work beautifully evokes.

A Literary World

Literature plays an important role in the portrait of Aura and the life she lived with Francisco. A well-known short story discussed by Francisco, "Axolotl" by Julio Cortázar, offers an important portrait of how people may attempt to know one another. The short story centers on a man's desire to see axolotls, the beautiful, mysterious, endangered amphibians. Also known as Mexican salamanders and Mexican walking fish (though they are not fish), axolotl are native to only central Mexico, specifically Lake Xochimilco and Lake Chalco. The latter no longer exists, and the former is an ecosystem polluted and threatened by the urban growth of Mexico City. Axolotls survive in captivity, and Cortázar's story takes place in Paris, where the protagonist visits the axolotls in the Jardin de Plantes. He stares at them daily until he eventually starts to see from their perspective, and one day he finds himself looking *out* through the eyes of the axolotl, at a man staring at them through the glass. This is the kind of transformation that Francisco seeks via Aura's writings and perhaps from his own writing of the book; he wants to look at Aura so intently that he can enter her consciousness. The reference to Cortázar's story appears early in the narrative and serves to frame the memoir; the narrator continues to evoke the relationship between Aura and the amphibian. At one point he refers to her as possessing "an axolotl gaze," a phrase that suggests that she is the specimen he studies (148). Axolotls, like Aura, are magical and disappearing Mexican creatures. When Aura and Francisco visit Paris for the first time they attempt to see the axolotls at the Jardin de Plantes but are told that they have been moved to another location. She writes in her journal, "Où sont les axolotls?" (Where are the axolotls?) (6). The phrase becomes an invocation of loss, the cry of someone searching for a beauty he or she knows exists but cannot see. The story of the axolotls then functions as an intertextual device that incorporates Latin American literature and ecology while offering the story of Francisco and Aura a structure and theme tied to larger literary and cultural traditions.

Literary references are appropriate given that both of the protagonists are writers. Francisco is a professional writer while Aura is pursuing a Ph.D. in literature, and later an M.F.A. in creative writing, during their relationship. A literary event was what brought the two together, as they met at a *presentación de libro* (book launch) in which Francisco was a participant and Aura a guest of the author, José Borgini. As mentioned earlier references to fictional writers such as Borgini are interspersed with those of living writers, including Salman

Rushdie, who was present at the dinner Francisco and Aura attended after the *presentación*. Excerpts from Aura's diaries and unpublished writings illuminate both the sense of Aura as a writer as well as the tragedy of her untimely death. Chapter 7 consists entirely of three epigraphs, all sections of short stories by Aura. After each epigraph we are told that the text comes from "an unfinished short story by Aura Estrada" (69). This line is repeated three times on the page and by the third time it has become unnecessary. The repetition, however, forces us to confront her untimely death over and over again, just as her husband, family, and friends must. Moreover, the use of these texts as epigraphs drives home the idea of a life cut short. Epigraphs are used to open sections of literary works; they do not usually compose the entirety of a text. When Goldman has chapter 7 contain *only* epigraphs, we are given an image of a literary piece that like Aura's life, has been unnaturally cut off.

As a writer the grieving husband also turns to books to understand and illustrate his grief. Francisco voraciously consumes books on mourning and mentions in particular Sigmund Freud's essay "Mourning and Melancholia." He explains to readers that he is unable to fulfill Freud's exhortation to accept death, saying that he did not want to accept Aura's death, or be "cured" of his response to it (184). Though he does not name it, he also refers to the most well-known description of stages of mourning, Elisabeth Kubler Ross's five stages of grief. He refers explicitly to the second stage, anger, although mostly to describe how quickly the stage passed for him. Exemplifying the importance of literature for both Aura and Francisco, the narrator also shows particular interest in his dead wife's books. While the narrator obsesses over Aura's possessions—her wedding dress, her face creams, her hairbrush and hat—her books are also special to him. He rereads books that she owned and which were important to her, such as Malcolm Lowry's *Under the Volcano* (a novel, not coincidentally set in Mexico), as yet another means of remembering and embodying her.

Along with reading literary texts to understand and cope with his own grief, Francisco expresses his grief through literary references. He tells readers of several tattoos that he gets in the years following Aura's death. One is the excerpt of a poem by Henry King, bishop of Chichester. He has the excerpt tattooed just below his collarbone in "tight cursive script" (192). The excerpt he includes is short: "ev'ry Howre a step toward Thee" (192). As he goes over the entire poem with his new lover, Ana Eva, he explains that the poem "gave [him] a way to talk to Ana Eva about what had happened" (192). King's words do what Francisco himself cannot, allowing him to communicate with others. Goldman also compared Aura to another literary wife, Queen Hermione of Shakespeare's *The Winter's Tale*. Speaking of how his attempt to re-create her was understood as an attempt to fill her wedding dress, which hung as an altar in their Brooklyn bedroom, Goldman wrote how he imagined that if only he could produce "the right sequence of words," he might walk into their bedroom to "find Aura restored to life like the statue of Queen Hermione in the last act of *The Winter's Tale,* standing there in her wedding dress and wondering why she was wearing it."[15] While as a novelist Goldman did not have a nonfiction guide in terms of how to craft the book, these references indicate that themes of death, loss, and restoration abound in literature.

Francisco appropriately characterizes himself and Aura in relation to literary texts, and the book alludes to a larger genre of literature and rhetoric not commonly associated with mourning—that of a criminal defense. After the loss of Aura, Francisco is overcome with both grief and guilt. The latter is of course exacerbated by the accusations levied against him by Aura's family, namely her mother and uncle. The defense that Francisco mounts seems directed at three audiences: himself, Aura's family, and his readership, and it relies on a language of criminality, references to famous criminals, and analyses of motivations and perspectives of those involved. In terms of the language of criminality, Francisco often assumes a self-exculpatory tone, and self-consciously so. Just after relating Aura's final words—"No quiero morir"—the narrator steps back and evaluates what he has just told his readers. "Did that sound self-exculpating? Is this the kind of statement I should prohibit myself from making?" (17). These questions indicate that he is under investigation and allude to the charges brought against him by Aura's family. He seems to recover himself and recognizes that he is not actually on trial. However, the lack of a criminal trial does not alleviate guilt; rather it potentially makes it worse as it is the grieving husband who must justify his thoughts and actions to himself. Francisco continues, "I need to stand nakedly before the facts; there's no way to fool this jury that I am facing. It all matters, and it's all evidence" (17). The jury that Francisco is facing is his own conscience, and it is no less a severe witness than a jury in a criminal case. Here the use of the language of a criminal trial references the charges that Francisco faced after Aura's death while also evidencing how these charges were reproduced within himself so that he had to defend himself not only to Aura's family or investigators, but to his own self.

Aura's family's suspicion and mistrust of Francisco is matched by his own thoughts about his culpability. As he pores over the details of their relationship he thinks about what could have prevented her death. Of course the very trip to Oaxaca, where Aura was fatally wounded, is an aspect that he considers. Why, he asks himself, did they not instead choose to vacation in the Yucatán, in Tulum, where they had vacationed earlier in their relationship? He then answers his own question; "Because I couldn't afford to rent a cottage for two weeks in Tulum, though I could in Oaxaca" (141). The more accessible, tourist-friendly Tulum is financially out of reach on Francisco's writer's salary. The implication here is that if Francisco made more money, they would not have had to go on a cheaper vacation, and Aura would be alive. Here the narrator echoes the author's description of the work; Goldman explained: "In this novel, I prosecute myself."[16] Finally the entertaining of self-blaming thoughts echoes Freud's description of melancholia. Freud wrote that melancholia is distinguished by, among other things, "self-reproaches and self-revilings" and "culminates in a delusional expectation of punishment."[17] Knowing that the narrator read Freud's work on the subject, "Mourning and Melancholia," suggests that the very shape of his grief may have been impacted by well-known descriptions of mourning. Taken together Francisco's self-prosecution, self-blame, and self-anguish contribute to the emotional depth and pain of the work while also inscribing the narrator and the work within larger literary and nonliterary discourses.

The Inevitability of Death and Mourning

Throughout the novel Francisco cannot help but wonder to what extent Aura's death is linked to their life together. Written as it is from the standpoint of the present and future, after Aura has passed, the entire narrative has an air of inevitability to it. Readers know that the story of their relationship will end with her tragic death, and thus, as Francisco narrates their meeting and time together, we follow him in his musings regarding at what point both of their fates were sealed. Often the inevitability of Aura's death is tied directly to Francisco with the latter channeling death itself; he suggests that the very moment he and Aura met foretold her destiny. When he describes their meeting in New York City he tells how he participated in a panel about the recent publication of a fellow author and then met Aura at the reception. He relates the first words they exchanged: "Hola! I said . . . she responded, Hola. (Hello! Meet your death. Hello, my death.)" (43). The reminder of Aura's impending death is unnecessary, excessive even. The too-cheery mimicry of death's words (Hola!/Hello!) portrays death as a presence from the start of their relationship. Furthermore, by having Aura greet death ("Hello, my death") Francisco suggests that she was aware, and perhaps accepting, of the role he would play in her life. Of course Francisco was not aware of the presence of death at their initial meeting; nevertheless, as he tells their story he must consider the importance of things he did not recognize at the time. Consequently, he cannot help but speculate regarding the significance of small details that at the time seemed inconsequential. He recalls a series of incidents in which he and Aura were separated by forces outside of their control. These include long customs lines they encountered when reentering the United States from Mexico when Francisco would clear customs with the U.S. citizens and then wait for Aura as she passed through "the much slower line for foreign visitors" (169). He remembers also an afternoon when Aura was momentarily trapped in an elevator in Columbia University and another time she mistook the subway stop where they were supposed to meet, leading them both to wait for the other in vain. Looking back the present-day narrator thinks of these as "moments of temporary separation and absence and even loss that were like little rehearsals for what was coming" (170). The vantage point of the present makes Francisco reconsider the significance of seemingly ordinary events in light of Aura's death.

Many of Francisco's premonitions are specific to potential fatalities in Mexico. The summer before she died, Francisco and Aura vacationed with friends on another beach in Oaxaca, San Agustinillo, just adjacent to Mazunte and an area marked by more dangerous waves. There another acquaintance told a story about a friend who had drowned some years earlier on an another Pacific Coast beach. The next day the acquaintance panicked at feeling a strong current around him and shouted for help. Aura dove in to swim the slightly embarrassed man to safety. On another earlier trip to Mexico, Francisco relates how a coconut from a tree in the courtyard of a hotel fell inches from his head. They joked that he could have easily been killed had it landed on his head. These stories have several implications. The anecdote about swimming, in which a man was not threatened although swimming in an area known for dangerous waves, serves as a counterpoint to the story of Aura's death—in which she was fatally injured in an area known to be safe for swimming. The result is to drive home the idea that none of us ever really knows how close we may be to danger and death. In addition, both of these stories suggest that perhaps it was Aura's proximity to others, namely Francisco, that endangered her. From this perspective perhaps the wave that killed her was not meant for her but for someone else.

Interestingly the possibility that the wave was not meant for Aura but for Francisco is never entertained by the narrator. Rather he suggests the opposite, referring to the wave that fatally injured her as "her wave." As part of his process of mourning, Francisco conducts research on waves, going so far as to send video of waves in Mazunte to a marine research institute in New Zealand (315). When he thinks back on their trip, he considers that the wave that killed Aura was already building as they journeyed to Mazunte. Specifically, he considers where the wave may have been as they lay in separate beds in a hostel in Oaxaca City, days before she was killed. Rewriting that moment, he asks, "that night, as we slept, where was Aura's wave in its long journey to Mazunte? Having done some research on waves since, I'm certain that that wave already existed" (306). Francisco cannot help but rewrite these days, writing Aura's wave into the story. Rather than wait for the moment when the wave would enter the story itself, the moment Aura dove into it, Francisco introduces it earlier, like a character that we must get to know in bits and pieces. In addition, referring to the wave as "Aura's" solidifies the destiny of the wave; it already belonged exclusively to her.

If Aura's death is portrayed as something unavoidable, even predictable, so too is the failure of her husband's various attempts to cope with her death. Francisco's mourning often assumes difficult, contradictory, and self-destructive forms. He describes sleeping with several young Mexican women in the years after Aura's death, including one of her best friends. These actions may be difficult to accept for readers; the narrator does not offer excuses but does gesture toward explanations. In terms of his relationship with two of Aura's best friends, one of whom he sleeps with and another with whom he makes brief, mad plans to run away to Mexico, Francisco explains: "We were all trying to find Aura in each other" and looking for "the embrace of someone who understood" (182). Despite these impulsive actions, Francisco stresses the very constant, even ordinariness of his grief. No matter who he slept with, he explains, he "felt the same . . . every morning, the same darkness and sadness, the same memories, images" (177). Francisco's actions and behavior may vary, but his grief remains.

Francisco grieves not only the loss of Aura, but the loss of her, and their collective, future. A few months after Aura's death, Francisco notices an elderly woman in their Brooklyn neighborhood and is forced to confront the fact that Aura will never grow old. The thought, he writes, "was like a silent bomb," and he contemplates the reality that Aura will "never get to look back on her own long life" (10). Francisco mourns the loss of Aura's future, a future that he poetically indicates would include a reflection on the past. This future-not-to-be that Francisco mourns includes himself and the plans that he and Aura had for their life, including their plans to have a child. The two had already selected potential names—Bruno for a boy, Natalia for a girl—and Francisco determines that they would have had a girl and that she would have been born in early 2009, about a year and a half after Aura died. He fixates on these details so thoroughly that he tattoos a birth date, 17/1/09, and "Natalia" on his forearm. In the time that passes between Aura's death and the imagined birth of Natalia, Francisco continues to include their unborn child in his life. When he marks the second New Year's Eve without Aura, he invents an alternative reality in which he imagines "Aura's belly . . . growing huge . . . Natalia's birth only seventeen days away" (202). Later when Aura's friends ask if he is OK with them naming their daughter Aura he says of course and then notes how incredible it was that "many of Aura's friends were having babies, just around when we were having Natalia!" (205). The specificity surrounding the date Natalia would be born is striking but is also a part of his process of grieving. Deciding the date of Natalia's birth is also a way of deciding when she would die; when January 2009 comes and goes without a child, he must confront the reality of Aura's death and the nonexistence of their child. This exercise reflects a taking control of his life; unlike the date of Aura's death, which he did not see coming, he is able to prepare for the date of Natalia's nonbirth. Once January 2009 passes, Francisco does not mention Natalia again and is able to prepare for the next important date, July 2009, when he will return to Mazunte for the two-year anniversary of Aura's death.

Mexico

The frequent back-and forth-movement from Mexico to the United States and back again mimics the processes of memory and grief in which Francisco is involved but also emphasizes the important role of Mexico. The country plays such a significant role in Aura and Francisco's relationship, their lives together, and his subsequent mourning that we may understand the country as a character in the novel. As a character Mexico is complex, expansive, dark, and beautiful. After their brief meeting in New York City, the two discover each other, by coincidence, in a rundown bar in a middle-class neighborhood of Mexico City. Francisco writes that they ran into each other at El Mitote, "a dingy bohemian and cokehead hangout on the edge of the Condesa. I was drinking at the bar with my friends . . . and there she was, standing before me. Hello again, my death" (120). He invites her out for a drink the next night, taking her to a much nicer restaurant and bar. He tells readers: "I'm sure I wasn't the first guy to have tried to impress her by inviting her [to the San Angel Inn], but at least she wouldn't think I hung out only in dumps like El Mitote" (120–21). The great city has facilitated their coming together and is used by the narrator as a means of characterizing himself, Aura, and his own aspirations.

Of course Mexico plays the largest role in Aura's death, and here the description of the last days of Aura's life coincide with other important aspects of the text, including its structure and its use of premonition. As the book draws to a close, the pace seems to quicken. Readers know that when Francisco begins to narrate his and Aura's vacation to Mazunte, we are nearing the story of her death. The narrative ceases to engage in longwinded descriptions, there are fewer back-and-forths between the story and the characters, no detours into descriptions of Aura's personality or her and her mother's relationship. Nevertheless, the narration of the days leading up to Aura's death are full of prescient details. He finally discloses to readers, for example, why he bought her a turquoise coffee press from Starbucks (because she had left her other one on a bus). At this point every detail feels significant.

Mazunte lies amid a strip of beach between two small cities in Oaxaca: Puerto Escondido and Puerto Ángel. Other nearby beaches include Zipolite, Ventanilla, and San Agustinillo. Mazunte is located near these beaches and is distinguished by its calmer waters. Francisco explains: "Mazunte is famously situated in a curving cove that impedes the waves rolling in from the ocean enough to diminish their size, momentum, and strength, its considered safe for swimmers. . . . You take your life into your hands when you swim at Ventanilla, to say nothing of Puerto Escondido or, father down the coast, Zipolite, notorious for its riptides and known as la Playa de la Muerte" (the beach of death) (299). Francisco presents the safety of Mazunte as relative, and indeed beaches such as Zipolite have frequent stories of drowning deaths, often U.S. or Canadian tourists. Francisco's explanation here, which reads as both an after-the-fact defense of the actions they all took as well as an in-the-moment explanation to Aura's friend Mariana why she should not be scared to join them, only sets the stage for what is to come.

When he returns to Mazunte a year after Aura's death, Francisco in many ways retraces the journey that she took in her dying day. He departs from Newark, taking the same flight to Mexico City that he and Aura had taken at the start of their trip. He wants to be in Mazunte on the anniversary of her death but then fly that same day back to Mexico City to attend a memorial mass at a church the next day. Goldman explained the placing of this section of the novel at the end as part of the process of writing. "Recounting that was horrible," he explained. He had to force himself to continue writing in order to finish it and was able to do so only by writing that entire section in one day; he finished at two in the morning and then put the writing aside for months.[18] In its final pages Francisco relinquishes Aura to Mexico, reflecting the character's and author's new relationship with the country. The author explained: "people don't really feel that a country is theirs until they've buried someone there. And burying Aura in Mexico has made it really sacred to me. I can't imagine cutting myself off from it."[19] In the narrative Francisco tattoos a broken heart over his own heart; above it is the date of Aura's death, 25/7/2007, and below it the phrase "hecho en México" (made in Mexico). What is "made" in Mexico remains ambiguous; the verb may refer to the country that birthed Aura as well as the country that killed her; the phrase occurring below the image of a broken heart also suggests that Francisco's own heart was made and unmade in Mexico. Rather than viewing the country as a place that robbed him of his wife, the author suggests that his current relationship with Mexico allows him to remain connected to Aura.

In Summary

Goldman's novel is the most recognized form that his grieving for his wife took, but it is not the only. True to both of their careers as writers, Goldman has worked to preserve Estrada's memory in specifically literary ways. In the years following her death, he helped to translate and publish her writing. In the spring of 2009 the literary journal *Zoetrope* published a special issue, featuring Latin American writers, in which a short story, "The Open Secret," written by Estrada and translated by Goldman, appeared. In 2010 her unpublished writings were released in a collection entitled *Mis días en Shanghai* (*My Shanghai Days*). Speaking of this work, and the ways that it contrasted the portrait of the widower in *Say Her Name,* Goldman noted that he was "a superb widower," who "honored [Estrada] every day."[20] The author also founded the Aura Estrada Prize, a monetary prize for a female Latin American writer under the age of thirty-five who writes in either English or Spanish. As a friend of Aura's noted in a moving piece in the Spanish-language literary journal *Letras Libras,* as of 2012 Aura would have been too old to receive the prize.[21] The biannual prize was first awarded in 2009, and it includes a stipend of $10,000 and the opportunity to reside in a writer's residence for up to two months (the residences are available in the United States, Mexico, and Italy).

Say Her Name is understandably unique within Goldman's larger body of work. Still its inclusion of autobiographical details and its portrayal of transnational (Mexican-U.S.) lives have much in common with earlier works. We may also understand the work as a bridge between his earlier and more recent texts. *Say Her Name* is the only book to defy a clear genre category, straddling fiction and memoir as it does. Goldman has continued aspects of *Say Her Name* in his current life and writing. For one, mentions of Aura are included in many of his more recent works. In addition, he continues to reside largely in Mexico City, splitting his time between Mexico City and Brooklyn, from where he commutes to teach at Trinity College in Hartford, Connecticut. It is this last aspect, Goldman's devotion to Mexico—his adopted homeland and Aura's birthplace—that carries over most prominently from *Say Her Name* to his most recent work, *The Interior Circuit: A Mexico City Chronicle.*

CHAPTER 7

Around Mexico

The Interior Circuit

Goldman's most recent book, *The Interior Circuit: A Mexico City Chronicle,* is his first book-length work in the genre of chronicle, or *crónica.* However, this nonfiction text also reads like a culmination of his two previous books, the nonfiction account of political murder, *The Art of Political Murder: Who Killed the Bishop?,* and the fictionalized portrait of grief and mourning, *Say Her Name.* Important elements of both of those works, namely crime, the genre of nonfiction, and personal healing, form the core of Goldman's chronicle. In addition, Goldman's publication of an English-language chronicle, a genre little known in the United States but well known in Latin America, reflects the transnationalism that marks all his work.

Mexico City has been an important part of Goldman's life, including his writing life, for several decades. An essay, "Mexico DF," published over a decade earlier, contains many of the same elements of *The Interior Circuit.* In the essay Goldman explained that his apartment in Mexico City is the "country house" to which he retreats, dividing his time (as he still does) between Mexico City and Brooklyn. (Goldman, "Mexico DF," 105) His origins in the city run deep; he was likely conceived there, readers learn, after a Guatemalan archbishop "ruled that [his] mamita could not marry a Jew in any church under his divine jurisdiction," leading his parents to marry in a side chapel of the Metropolitan Cathedral with "rented bridesmaids" (106). Goldman also tackled in the essay questions of belonging and authenticity. He proffered that he does not "claim to know much about Mexico . . . the city, the country, even the people," although his insights regarding everything from the layout of the city, to its history, to its "iron-clad race-based class system" clearly belie a deep familiarity (108, 110). He has also made light of the question of authenticity that so often plagues "foreigners," writing honestly that he lives in La Condesa, a comfortable neighborhood "everyone makes fun of but that many want to live in" (109). He also has confronted one of Mexicans' most beloved terms of derision, the adjective "fresa," which literally translates to strawberry but in Mexican Spanish is used to describe a person or thing that is uppity or snobby. He gently complains about the popular tendency for people to go on "about how this person or that person or that place is so horribly fresa while pretending that they themselves aren't as fresa as everyone else" (110). When he cheerfully admits that he is also fresa he exposes the hypocrisy of a label so easily applied to everyone and everything except its speaker. Still he loves living in the fresa-obsessed city. The essay appropriately ends where *The Interior Circuit* picks up, with an image of an elderly Mexican man learning to drive circling a roundabout in Goldman's neighborhood.

Goldman was inspired by the elderly student driver he spied in his essay, and the commitment to learning is revived when the author determined to learn to drive in the city in the years after Aura's death. Learning to drive for Goldman was of course a way for him to continue to process his grief over the loss of his young wife, Aura Estrada. As he explained in a short piece published in *Virginia Quarterly,* this most recent book is "in some ways a sequel" to *Say Her Name.*[1] When the book opens, it is 2012, five years after Aura's death. Goldman's driving lesson commemorates the five-year anniversary of Aura's tragic accident in the beach town of Mazunte, Oaxaca, Mexico, an accident that led to her death twenty-four hours later, in July 2007. The fifth anniversary of Aura's death is significant also because it marks that Goldman had now been mourning Aura longer than he'd known her. Learning to drive was not so much moving on for Goldman as it was moving into a different stage of mourning. As he explained in *Say Her Name,* Mexico, Aura's native country, became a sacred place to him after her death. Learning to know Mexico in a new, deeper way, has furthered and maintained his connection with his lost wife.

As Goldman got to know parts of Mexico City, he introduced these parts to his reader and delved deeper into the history, culture, and social life as well as the crime and politics of the area. These latter two issues are the focus of the second half of the chronicle. In this section Goldman veered to a different track as he investigated the abduction and disappearance of a dozen patrons of an after-hours club in May 2013. While Mexico City has gained a reputation as a violent city in recent years, Goldman explained that this crime, which occurred in the early-morning hours of a Sunday and in a populous, middle-class section of the city, was anomalous. The intensity with which Goldman became interested in the case, known as the Heavens case (after the name of the nightclub,

After Heavens), is also an index of his growth and grief. The entire book spans two summers, the summer of 2012, when he began his driving lessons, and the summer of 2013, which he spent investigating the crime.

Chronicle

The English-language subtitle of the book, "A Mexico City Chronicle," references a well-established Spanish-language genre, the *crónica*. *Crónicas* have a specific history and function within Latin American letters. As the name indicates, they are meant to record events, people, and places and are often first-person singular accounts of a particular encounter told in such a way as to introduce a large, likely remote, audience to this new location. Thus it is no surprise that many critics have viewed the accounts of the Conquest of the Americas as the first *crónicas*. These accounts included Columbus's letters to the king of Spain as well as books written by men who accompanied the Spanish soldiers, such as Bernal Díaz del Castillo, the author of *The True History of the Conquest of New Spain*. However, the contemporary genre is more closely related to late nineteenth- and early twentieth-century works by José Martí of Cuba and Rubén Darío of Nicaragua; these two writers are the best-known representatives of *crónica modernista* (modern chronicle).[2] Despite the genre's Latin American roots, Jennifer Harford Vargas and Monica Hanna explained that *crónicas* also have a close relation to the English-language tradition of advocacy journalism. Both *crónicas* and long-form journalism move beyond a focus on objectivity to offer in-depth portraits of people or issues (65). In addition, *crónicas,* like advocacy journalism, often focus on pressing social issues of the day. U.S. Latina/o writers who utilize the genre often do so in their focus on migration; this is the case for writers such as Sonia Nazario, Rubén Martínez, and Luis Alberto Urrea. Exemplifying the use of the genre by writers from a variety of backgrounds, Nazario and Martínez are journalists while Urrea is also a poet and novelist. The fact that *crónica* employs aspects of fiction—a stylized voice, the inclusion of the writer him- or herself in the work—makes it an in-between genre that is in fact an appropriate metaphor for U.S. Latina/os. Chronicles, and their authors, are often both "inside" and "outside" their story, a position that Latina/os, as well as other ethnic minorities and migrants, may experience in their relationship to the United States. While the Latina/o chronicle draws from the Latin American tradition and often places it within significant U.S. phenomena, namely migration, Harford Vargas and Hanna noted that it has a few distinguishing characteristics. More so than its Latin American counterpart, Latina/o chronicle emphasizes "the individual and cultural repercussions of lives lived across national borders" (66). These experiences may be expressed through transnational references and connections made between the United States and Latin America (66). Goldman's use of this genre indicates his deep connection to both English- and Spanish-language literary traditions. That he utilized a Latin American genre for a book written in English aptly captures the binational orientation of the author. Where he has differed from some of his U.S. Latina/o peers is that *The Interior Circuit* does not focus on Latin American migrants in the United States (as does work by Nazario, Urrea, and others). However, the work fulfills characteristics of the genre in its commitment to a nuanced, multifaceted portrait that includes insight on politics, culture, and history and includes the author's own perspectives and experiences.

Popular Reception

Given that chronicle is an underexamined genre in English-language publishing, it is not surprising that few reviewers note this aspect of the text. Rather the North American press has largely commented on the text's content, namely its portrait of violence and political corruption in Mexico. In some ways this is unfortunate and contradicts one of the book's central ideas; the nightclub killing was notable precisely because it marked a moment of violence within the capital city, which had largely been considered safe. The fact that the killing reflected a shift, or a return to an earlier period of violence, is missed by the *New York Times* review that suggests that "if things were really that bad in Mexico City, even our battle-scarred author might think twice about living there."[3] This comment suggests that Goldman's portrait of violence in Mexico City is hyperbolic while also playing into the idea of a place that is too violent for a U.S. citizen to live. That the book is a "love letter" to the city was captured by NPR's Arun Rath. In an interview with Rath, Goldman credited the city with helping him to get through "a very difficult period in [his] life," the death of his wife, Aura Estrada. Well-aware of negative stereotypes of the city, Goldman has been careful to correct such ideas. He explained that in the late 1990s the city deserved its reputation for lawlessness and violence. However since 1998 the city has been "uniquely well-governed," and by 2010 the crime rate was on par with New York City's.[4]

Goldman addressed the violence in Mexico head on in both specific and general terms. He told of a murder that happened in his neighborhood in 2008 and then offered a slew of statistics concerning crime in the region. While, as he stated in his NPR interview, Mexico City has a homicide rate equal to that of New York City, several Mexican cities have much higher rates (including Ciudad Victoria, Cuernavaca, and Monterrey), and the country as a whole has a murder rate per capita of 19.4 out of 100,000 (the United States' is 6.2). Significantly almost 99 percent of crimes are not solved, although in the capital city the rate of impunity is about 50 percent. (Goldman, Interior Circuit, 49) Goldman blamed much of this crime on the drug cartels whose power impacts large swaths of society. For example, Mexico is an incredibly dangerous place to practice journalism, and newspapers often engage in explicit self-censorship to protect themselves.

Other reviews were much more positive, such as that written by the *Los Angeles Times'* David Ullin, who called the book "sneakily brilliant."[5] Ullin rightfully credited the book for mixing genres, explaining that it is "part travelogue, part memoir, part reportage on Mexican politics and the scourge of narco-terrorism," but he seemed to ignore the book's subtitle and credited Goldman with "[creating] . . . a form" rather than employing the use of *crónica*. Ullin however accurately captured how the book unites its two foci, the death of Aura and the After Heavens case. He explained that the "genius" of the book is its ability to "link Goldman's grief for Aura to the grief of all these families and indeed of Mexico."[6] Indeed Goldman managed to merge his own mourning with that of the city and country he so loves such that the book becomes a collective experience of grief and loss. The author has guided readers as he considered the loss of Aura, the loss of countless victims of narco-violence, and the loss of the protective bubble that was once Mexico City. The book has received effusive praise from U.S. Latina/o critics, including authors Daniel Alarcón and Rubén Martínez. Alarcón named the book "a marvel," and Martínez named it "an indispensable contribution to the growing body of artistic representations of Mexico's recent years of darkness."[7] These assessments carry particular weight, and they point to Goldman's belonging among a vibrant group of contemporary Latina/o authors who have also crossed linguistic and national borders: Martínez is well known for his deeply researched and penetrating portrait of migration in *Crossing Over,* while Alarcón, like Goldman, is a binational author who writes about Latin America in English and is the executive producer of the Spanish-language radio program *Radio Ambulante,* which has featured Goldman several times.

Part One: Knowing Self

As mentioned earlier the first half of the book revolves around Goldman learning to drive in the city. Learning to drive was a way of taking control of his life and over his own process of mourning. He explained to Arun Rath: "in the five years of grief I hadn't driven a car anywhere, which seemed to me a metaphor of the sort of listlessness and loneliness of grief."[8] Learning to drive was a means of learning to navigate among his own feelings and experiences. Neither process, navigating the city or his own feelings, involved a completely linear process but rather brought developments that he could not have predicted. On the day that his lessons were to culminate, he took a wrong turn and ended up on a street adjacent to the UNAM—the Universidad Nacional Autónoma de México (the National Autonomous University of Mexico). The world-renowned, sprawling UNAM is where his late wife, Aura Estrada, studied, and Goldman ended up on a street called Calle Facultad de Filosofía y Letras (Department of Philosophy and Literature), which is what Aura studied. Finding himself at a place where Aura would have been fifteen years earlier allowed Goldman to connect with his wife and also say goodbye to her again; he described the moment as "an embrace and a goodbye."[9] Moreover the moment, because it was unexpected, was much more meaningful "than when I finally reached my destination."[10] In this way Goldman's narrative fulfills the cliché that a journey is much more important than any destination.

While the narrative centers on the summer of 2012, much of the work is devoted to Goldman excavating parts of himself, or the person that he was in decades past. The fact that he has had such a long-standing relationship with the city facilitates this process of reflection. Even though he explained that he had signed up for driving lessons, he had in fact driven in the city previously, notably on a memorable night when he drunkenly drove his friend's car home from a party. Goldman recalled that he felt as though he had "mastered driving in the DF" that night and recalled "a euphoric ride, racing down Avenida Insurgentes Sur, passing cars, an impression of lights bursting and streaming past and vanishing behind" (8–9). While he admitted that his inebriated state and night blindness meant he should not have been driving at all, he also noted that since that night, he had felt a challenge to learn to drive in the city (8–9). When he neared the end of his week of driving lessons, at which point, at the urging of his teacher he has abandoned his goal of learning to drive stick shift, he recalled his drunken night but in a way that placed insurmountable distance between that time and the present of the book. "Who was the person who'd driven that night?" he asked himself. "He seemed remote from me now. Would I ever drive like that again? I couldn't imagine even trying to" (102). Whereas once he had been motivated by a desire to recapture, even extend, the experience he had driving that night, he now realized that he was no longer the same person. Comparing his past and present experiences driving, which occur twelve years apart, allowed him the opportunity to compare his past and then present selves.

Part of the person that he has now become, of course, is one without his beloved wife. In a touching passage that illustrates the irrevocable alterations Aura and her death have made in his life, Goldman recalled some of the humorous games the two of them would play. He explained that they would often attempt to caption the comics that occurred at the back of the *New Yorker* magazine:

"we'd always invent captions that seemed pretty clever to me, though we never submitted any of them. After Aura was gone, whenever I looked at that page, no funny caption ever came to me" (106). Of course mourning in Mexico did allow Goldman the opportunity to discuss the now well known (and well culturally appropriated) Mexican holiday of Day of the Dead. Perhaps foreseeing the extent to which the holiday would continue to grow in popularity outside of the nation and become highly associated with Mexican culture, he insisted that suggesting that Mexicans have a special relationship with death based on the holiday is like asserting that, because of Thanksgiving, the United States is a nation of "turkey whisperers" (115). However, he does contrast U.S. and Mexican ways of mourning. While a friend, a writer, in New York once told him that he (the friend) was envious because now Goldman "had a tragic but beautiful love story attached to [his] life," friends in Mexico displayed neither such selfishly ignorant responses nor awkwardness that led, for example, other friends to avoid inviting Goldman to their homes. "In Mexico, I never sensed that anyone felt obligated to say or display anything in particular in the presence of a 'bereaved person,' and nobody stopped inviting me anywhere" (125). Goldman's reflections on his own experiences of mourning in Mexico offer another explanation for why the country was so important to him during this time: the physical space facilitated his relationship to Aura (even after her death), and the cultural landscape was more hospitable to a person in his grief-stricken state.

There are two main mechanisms through which Goldman's knowledge of himself and his knowledge of Mexico are linked in the text: Aura and maps of the city. As he recalled his experiences in Mexico City he wondered whether he ever could have encountered Aura at an earlier time. Speaking of living near an art space run by friends, Goldman supposed that he might have run into Aura there before they ever met since for a time she dated an artist who also frequented the space. He brought his knowledge of Mexican culture to bear when he went on to say that Aura, like many young Mexican women, was occasionally secretive about her past, which he explained as stemming from persistent misogyny that threatens to judge women who "behave even somewhat as any Mexican male is allowed" (43). The extended amount of time he has spent in Mexico has granted him further insight into his late wife's personality and mannerisms. Knowledge of Aura also comes from her friends, and this knowledge is again facilitated by Goldman's residence in the city. "That's become a part of living in Mexico City too; every now and then someone tells me something about the Aura she or he knew before I met her" (46). By living in Mexico, Goldman gained greater knowledge about Aura; this does not solve but has only facilitated his own processes of self-recovery. Because Aura and her loss is so significant in his life and because Aura is so connected to Mexico

City, Goldman has become convinced that the city holds a key to understanding more about his own loss. "I felt that there was a problem or riddle I had to solve and that somehow Mexico City, or something in my relationship to the city, held a solution" (9). While the problem he was looking to solve remains unspecified, it is clear that proximity to Aura has been important to him. Remaining in Mexico, going deeper into the culture and history, has allowed him to remain proximate to Aura and perhaps promised to allow him to move through his grief to a new state.

The Interior Circuit also touches on maps of the sprawling city, and here Goldman described how getting to know other aspects of the physical space was linked to getting to know deeper regions of his own conscience, life, or memories. The secret that he hoped to unlock is also discussed in relation to mastering the city spatially. He designed a driving game that, "almost like the I Ching," involved opening a city guidebook, the *Guia Roji,* to any page, putting his finger down randomly and then trying to drive to that destination (14). The *Guia Roji* functions as a literal map in the text, around which Goldman organized the narrative. After going into details about people—artists, friends, lovers—he used the *Guia* to locate himself. We are given a sense of the immensity of the city when he described that although he has moved apartments several times, for the past twenty years he has only ever lived within two squares of the *Guia*. He spent time in the neighborhood of Coyoacán, which owing to its being the neighborhood of the homes of Frida Kahlo and Leon Trotsky (the proximity between the homes is not coincidental as Kahlo and her husband, Diego Rivera, were supporters of the communist exile) is a tourist haven, but Goldman described it as possessing "an aura of hippie nostalgia" and "complacent culture of millionaire Communists" (29). He left Coyoacán for La Condesa, which at that time (the early 1990s) was a site that was "becoming" a neighborhood much in the way that the now trendy Brooklyn neighborhood of Williamsburg was becoming. He explained that he liked how much was within his reach in La Condesa—cantinas, art galleries, nightclubs, strip bars. Goldman has given us the exact location of his apartments according to the *Guia Roji* grid: "Since 1995 I've always lived within squares 168 and, only this year, 169" (32). Despite its reliance on the *Guia,* Goldman's book also includes metaphors of the good that can come from *not* following a clear route, something Goldman has been conscious of. Although he decided to take driving lessons in July, he did not start them until August, just one example of a plan not followed closely. The narrative likewise does not follow a clear schedule, and he commented, "I am taking a circuitous route through the summer of 2012, when it turned out that I didn't get to where I'd hoped to arrive quite by following the plan I'd laid out" (39).

The book includes Goldman's trademark humor, *chistes* (jokes) offered with no necessary explanation. He quoted his driver's manual: "Does a red light mean nothing? Unfortunately, this is a cultural problem of many people who live in Mexico" (36). He approached Mexico as both an insider and an outsider, someone who loves the city enough not to overly romanticize it while also acknowledging that he cannot know it as a native does. He wrote that he "wants to celebrate but also defend the city" (172). One of the things the city seems to offer him are endless opportunities to begin anew. On the opening pages of the book he described a scene he witnessed fifteen years earlier, when he spied another driving student, this one circling the Glorieta Citaltépetl, a roundabout near where he was living. Remembering the driver, who was in his seventies, reminded Goldman that "it wasn't too late" for him to overcome his various fears about driving in the city (traffic, dangerous weather, getting lost) (8).

While the summer of 2012 was focused on literal movement through the city, the period also included a momentous low: a beating by a group of young wealthy Mexicans, also known as *juniors*. Goldman and his friend Reyna had ended up on a party bus, a place that owing to class and age they did not belong, at the invitation of some Americans they had met at a bar. After a misunderstanding (likely Goldman's companion hitting on the young sister of one of the young men), the two were thrown off the bus, literally kicked off. Drunkenly Goldman invited a youth to fight but was swarmed by more than a dozen who kicked him nearly into unconsciousness on the pavement. In the days that followed, a friend helped him put this drunken night in perspective regarding the years he had lived since Aura: "It could also be a search for a rock bottom that is more bottom than the one you lived a few years ago" (167). He accepted his own culpability for the incident and allowed it to change him: "self-debasing calamity or brush with death and wake-up call, it changed everything" (168). While the incident itself is significant, careful readers will understand that Goldman was ready for this change. Prior to telling the story he discussed over a dozen other dangerous or near death threats he had survived. What distinguishes this night from, for example, the multiple muggings he has survived, is that he so carelessly placed himself in harm's way. This distinction of course means that he can make choices to avoid such situations in the future. He was ready not to move on but to move differently; as he himself said, the experience moved him to a "new circuito" (168).

Part Two: Knowing Mexico

The year in which the chronicle takes place, 2012, is personally and politically significant. As stated earlier, the year marked the five-year anniversary of Aura's death. But it also marked a significant shift in Mexico politics; it is the year that the PRI (Partido Institucional Revolucionario / Institutional Revolutionary Party) returned to power. The PRI famously, and corruptly, ruled Mexico for seventy years; they were finally voted out of office with the election of Vicente Fox, who represented the right-wing PAN, Partido Acción Nacional (National Action Party), in 2000. Goldman explained: the PRI "had been governing Mexico since 1929, its candidates' victories in presidential elections every six years abetted by widespread electoral fraud, until, in 2000, Vicente Fox Quesada of the rightist National Action Party (PAN) was selected president" (25). Mexican presidents serve for one term of six years; the PAN won again, although in a hotly contested election in 2006, at which point Felipe Calderón took office. When the PRI candidate, Enrique Peña Nieto (known commonly by his initials EPN), was elected in 2012, the election represented a return to a period of corruption that many Mexicans believed was over.

While one could assume that after decades in more or less continuous residence in the city, Goldman was well versed in Mexico's politics, he admitted that in fact he avoided knowledge of the political situation in his adopted land. "For years, I'd considered the DF my place of escape from, or my neutral place between, the two bordering countries where before I'd spent almost all my adult life: the United States and Guatemala, countries whose politics are impossible to ignore if you live in either, and that can exhaust, sour, and depress anybody" (66–67). He credited his interest in political events that summer to both his own general awakening to the world around him as well as his encounter with young people who were involved in student protests. These young people, of course, reminded him of Aura and how he imagined she might have responded to the political climate.

Thus one of the notable events from the summer that he recounted is the protest at the Universidad Iberoamericana (Iberoamerican University) and the subsequent media activism captured by the hashtag #YoSoy132. The author explained that in Mexico's rigidly classist education system, La Ibero, as it is called, is an elite Jesuit-sponsored university, a place not known for political activism and one where EPN, who the author noted, "looks like a Ken doll," might send his daughter (51). Thus when La Ibero erupted in protests against EPN it was surprising to all. The incident at La Ibero involved a frustrated presidential candidate letting down his guard and defending abuses committed by the Mexican state as "the legitimate use of force that corresponds to the state" (54). This force included the sending of hundreds of riot police to the town of Atenco in Mexico State in May 2006 (EPN was governor at the time). There the police faced off with unarmed protestors who were mobilizing against the proposed construction of a new airport that involved the expropriation of land. The police presence provoked two murders (both at the hands of police, one by a beating with batons) and the sexual assault of dozens of women. When EPN defended these actions the students erupted in anger, forcing him to flee the university. His exit was impeded, however, by the angry students, and at one point he and his security detail sought refuge in a men's bathroom. Goldman surmised: "No serious future biography of Enrique Peña Nieto or history of his presidency will be able to avoid mentioning that second-floor men's room" (55). Peña Nieto's supporters in the media responded by circulating the idea that the students who had protested were not actually university students but paid agitators; in response an Ibero student put out a call over social media for his peers to make videos affirming their identity as students (by displaying ID cards for example) and that they had participated in the protest. He received 131 videos, which he edited into one; adding his own he created 132 testimonies of student protestors. As Goldman explained it was surprising that students at a *fresa* school like La Ibero had agitated as they had.

The Ibero protest spawned a hashtag #YoSoy132 (I am 132), a reference to the 132 videos that students uploaded to document their participation in the protests; the personal testimonies were necessary to combat rumors by EPN-sympathetic media that it was not the students, but plants from a rival party, who had risen up against EPN. From this unlikely source a new student movement erupted as students from La Ibero united with those from the much larger and more politically radical UNAM as well as universities around the city. They even connected with student leaders from other countries, notably Camila Vallejo from Chile, where students had successfully pushed back against government attempts to add to the growth of for-profit education. The Mexican movement, like its Chilean counterpart, became a sign of general discontent with government leaders, with the specific addition in the Mexican context of a rejection of PRI corruption. Despite the significant movement, which Goldman participated in via attending meetings and participating in marches, the PRI candidate, EPN, was elected in December 2012. His election brought a somber note to the *crónica,* which increased when Goldman turned to the After Heavens case in 2013.

The second half of the *crónica* focuses on a case study of sorts, of the transformations that have marked Mexico City since 2012. In the summer of 2013, on May 26, a dozen people were kidnapped outside of a Mexico City nightclub. Dubbed a "*levantón*" because the group literally was lifted into thin air, the case was notable because it took place in an area heavily populated and popular with *chilangos* (as Mexico City natives are known) and foreigners alike. Goldman approached the case as a sign of the waning of Mexico City's exceptional status and one linked to the inauguration of EPN in 2012 as well as being the first real challenge of the current mayor of the city, Miguel Ángel

Mancera, who took office in early 2013. These two positions, mayor of Mexico City and president of the republic, are linked owing to a history of Mexico City mayors running for the national seat. The way that Mancera responded to the kidnapping, as well as how he handled his relationship with EPN, who is both from a different political party and broadly reviled by the Mexico City populace, became a way of gauging the feelings of the city and the country as a whole.

Goldman's investigations into the case were aided by a Spanish reporter, Pablo de Llano, who writes for *El País*. With de Llano, Goldman ventured into Tepito, the neighborhood all the disappeared were from. Tepito is an infamous neighborhood in Mexico; its role as a place of commerce dates back to the Conquest, when it was "a poor indigenous neighborhood . . . whose residents despised the Spaniards and were always looking for ways to dupe them" (191). According to the author, the area today is one of "pirates, contrabandists, gangs, gangsters, drug use, and drug peddling" as well as a labyrinth of a *tianguis* (markets) (192). Being from a poor and even criminal barrio is not, of course, a crime, and Goldman resisted and criticized media that played up the victims' birthplace. U.S. readers who are familiar with the ways in which media sometimes serve to criminalize victims, particularly victims of color and those from lower socioeconomic classes, will not be surprised by this happening to the victims of the After Heavens case. The city government leaked information to the press meant to cast doubt on the innocence of the victims largely because of their hailing from Tepito. Two of the disappeared were the sons of imprisoned gangsters, and one of the boys' grandmothers fought back against the tendency to slander a child for the crime of his father or for where he was born. The barrio is dangerous, Goldman reported her having said, but having a father who is a narco does not "diminish the importance of finding" the disappeared (198).

While Goldman and de Llano took the crime seriously, it is hard to believe that organized crime did not have something to do with the *levantón*. Similar to his work on the assassination of Archbishop Juan Gerardi, *The Art of Political Murder* (2007), Goldman considered various different angles. He relayed what was reported in mainstream Mexican news sources as well as newer online sources, and his own assessments were aided by those of his friends and colleagues. Fortuitously Goldman lived in the same apartment building as Marcel Ebrard, the most recent mayor of Mexico City, whose term in office ran from 2006 to 2012. In the first part of the book, Goldman credited Ebrard with continuing a tradition of successful governing of the city, lauding his initiatives to improve the quality of life of ordinary citizens through free skate rinks, public anthropological displays, and expansion of the Metrobús. In this second part he continued to consult members of Ebrard's security team who were almost always somewhere near the building. Ebrard is portrayed as an intelligent, realistic politician; of the security cameras that his administration had installed throughout the city, he mentioned to Goldman that they also watch over the police. Goldman described Mancera's administration as starkly different than Ebrard's; the new mayor embraced the reviled president EPN, placing him at odds with both his own predecessor as well as many of his own constituents.

The abduction of a dozen people in broad daylight could not have taken place without some significant planning and coordination. While the obvious people behind the crime are narcos (narco-traffickers or someone involved in any aspect of the drug trade), their operation in the city could not occur without the knowledge, if not condoning, of members of the police or government. On a national level, Mexico since 2006 has taken a new and disastrous tactic in the drug wars. Starting under former president Felipe Calderón, and at the urging of the United States, the Mexican state militarized the fight against the cartels. This strategy has been continued under EPN with disastrous consequences; "seventy thousand Mexicans have been killed and some twenty-seven thousand disappeared, effectively turning the whole country into a 'narco grave.'"[11] But Goldman was most concerned with the ramifications of the crime for Mexico City politics; he took several opportunities to query members of Ebrard's security detail on the crime. When he asked if the crime could have had political motives, if the PRI could have been behind it, if Mancera could have been involved, he was told simply, "Stranger things have happened in Mexico." (Goldman, Interior Circuit, 214) Indeed it is somewhat difficult for non-Mexican readers to fully understand the possibilities behind some of these scenarios. Why would the PRI be behind a mass kidnapping and murder? The idea is that the PRI wanted to destabilize the city so as to seize control over it. The fact that Mancera rules so differently than his PRD predecessors has granted evidence that he could be a PRI plant. Goldman maintained his relationship with Ebrard and his men while his colleague de Llano had sources within Mancera's government. The two compared sources. According to de Llano's source, Mancera did not have control of the judicial police, which led to a growing power by police-protected criminals; these criminals in turn were fighting among themselves for control over the city's drug markets. Goldman explained that the police in Mexico City are "an autonomous culture" who "*are* organized crime" (254–55). While it is difficult to determine who orchestrated the crime (if indeed it stemmed from powers within the government) Goldman passed along the perspective that the crime had "great political capital" and had become a "political weapon" (255). It seems undoubtable that some level of security forces had to have had knowledge of the crime; the *levantón* took place just blocks from the Ministry of Public Security, where the chief of police is headquartered; there were hundreds of police in the area. Goldman did trace this back to Mancera's rule when he pointed out that Mancera tapped as his head of the Ministry of Public Security a man who had worked in narco-controlled zones in northern Mexico; judicial employees from that area (including police) are "at least passively complicit" in the activities of the drug cartels (256). The fact that Mancera has placed prominent people in positions of power who do not inspire confidence, however, already suggests a weakness of his government; as Ebrard told Goldman, the mayor's job consists of two things—keeping the city secure, and governing in a way that is liberal and progressive. Working with corrupt police threatens both of those mandates.

Of course there is no doubt that Goldman was drawn to the After Heavens case, at least in part, owing to his own losses. His colleague Pablo de Llano has been the only reporter to seriously cover the loss that the families have suffered, which he has done through a photojournalism project. Owing to this de Llano and Goldman have been granted access to the grieving family members. In a touching moment he described understanding the seemingly illogical desire of Leticia Ponce, the mother of one of those abducted, to take her four-year-old granddaughter to a fountain in the city. Ponce is married to a narco who is in prison and whose criminal status is a possible motive behind the kidnapping of his son. Speaking to the author, Leticia told him she wants to join her granddaughter; she explained, "I want to get wet, I want to scream" (301). Goldman hugged her deeply, remarking at the strangeness of hugging the wife of an imprisoned narco, but also noted that he understands her pain. "I want to tell her, Believe me, I know, I understand. . . . Go and get wet in the fountain, go and scream!" (301).

His ability to offer empathy to Ponce also denotes the passage of time, and readers are able to see how Goldman changed in even the span of one year. When the sixth anniversary of Aura's death arrived, he was deep into his investigations of the After Heavens case, and he noted the date July 25 as the sixth anniversary of Aura's death and as the nearly two-month anniversary of the *levantón*. He even told his friends explicitly that he needed less support, remarking to his girlfriend, "I just don't need people to show me that kind of care or support anymore and don't want them to feel obligated" (204). He was referring specifically to his decision not to tell more people about the mass that was to be said in Aura's memory, and the remark was a clear-visioned assessment of his own altered state. He placed himself in relation to the families of the disappeared, recalling how terrified and helpless he felt during Aura's last hours. Goldman was able to connect his personal grief with that of Ponce and of Ponce's family, and in some ways this elevated his own mourning. He could offer her a different kind of understanding, and she him, even if she did not know it. Joining his grief with hers within this politically significant case was a way of also marking grief over the loss of a particular moment in time, a time when the city seemed less dangerous, before everything "ha cambiado" (has changed).

In August 2013 a mass grave was discovered in the municipality of Tlalmanalco, in neighboring México State. Although the discovery of the grave included contradictory information—authorities originally claimed the breakthrough was a result of collaboration between agencies but later said the grave was found accidentally—forensic evidence did eventually identify all the victims. The prosecution ruled that the kidnappings and murders were an act of revenge perpetuated by La Unión de Insurgentes against La Unión de Tepito. The motive was an earlier murder of another drug dealer, and thus the entire crime was due to a "turf war" between rival gangs (308). Although the targets may have been the two sons of imprisoned gangsters, committing a much larger murder may have been a way of sending a political message and of testing the Mancera government to see how it would respond. In the fall of that year several low-level gang members were arrested for the crime, but Goldman and de Llano continued to speculate that the crime could not have taken place without the complicity of higher-ups, including members of the police. As of 2016 twenty-two people had been found responsible for the crime.[12] Goldman ended by placing the case within the larger context of crime and impunity in Mexico, discussing the 2014 arrest of infamous leader of the Sinaloa Cartel, Joaquín "El Chapo" Guzmán, who may have negotiated his own arrest. A 2015 postscript discusses the "Mexican Autumn" of 2014, when a major movement erupted in response to the kidnapping, murder, and government cover-up of forty-three students from a rural teacher's school. The movement, which mobilized under the hashtag #Yamecansé (I'm tired), was covered by Goldman in a multipart series for the *New Yorker.*[13]

In Summary

The Interior Circuit is Goldman's most personal book. Speaking of the relationship between self, truth, and writing, he explained that "the stories one tells about oneself aren't necessarily true, of course, but I wanted this one to be as true as I could make it." (Goldman, Interior Circuit, 171) No doubt incorporating aspects of his life, Aura's life, and the current political situation contributed to this truth. Interestingly it is his least U.S.-centric text; the entirety of the text takes place in Mexico City, where Goldman interacts almost exclusively with Mexican writers, politicians, and journalists. In doing so Goldman has joined a larger community of U.S. Latina/o writers who write of and from Mexico.

Chicana/o authors, naturally, have a long tradition of exploring the country of their parents or grandparents; prime examples include Ana Castillo's novel *The Mixquiahala Letters,* Cherríe Moraga's poems and essays in *The Last Generation* and *Loving in the War Years,* and Sandra Cisneros's short stories and novel *Caramelo*. Cisneros, like Goldman, currently lives in Mexico, having recently moved to San Miguel de Allende, Guanajato. Younger writers also write of and from Mexico City, most prominently Daniel Hernández, whose time in the capital inspired his collection *Down and Delirious in Mexico City.* What is different between these writers and Goldman, of course, is that they are Mexican American or Chicana/o and presumably have some familial or cultural ties to the country that the Jewish Guatemalan American Goldman himself lacks. However, both Goldman himself and the city that he loves might push back against such narrow definitions of identity and belonging. Mexico City, one could say, does not itself belong only to the nation of México but is rather its own hybrid space. Moreover, Goldman's oeuvre encourages us to think more broadly about connections between people, places, and politics throughout the Western Hemisphere(s).

Finally, while *The Interior Circuit* offers a snapshot of Mexico City, it also reminds us that the city is constantly changing. Recently, in 2016, the city ceased being a Distrito Federal. Previously the city was known by this name—D.F.—a political designation akin to that of Washington, D.C. (District of Columbia) in the United States. To advertise the shift, the city was plastered with images and letters evoking its new name—CDMX—Ciudad de México (City of Mexico). The letters appeared in large pink print on the subway and on the side of buses and even as a sculpture in public space. The change represents the fact that the beautiful city, like its millions of dynamic inhabitants, continues shifting.

Conclusion

Goldman in the Global South

Francisco Goldman's career has brought him critical and popular success in a variety of genres: journalism, novels, and chronicle. He has drawn from his personal history and experiences, mainly his deep knowledge of Guatemala and Central America, to present a unique and necessary binational perspective on history, politics, and culture. His ability to "translate" Latin American phenomena to a U.S. audience facilitates transnational dialogue, while at the same time his own life and work encourage us to recognize that these hemispheric exchanges are not new. While the migration of people, business, and politics within the American hemisphere has been constant for the past several centuries, the landscape of the United States is currently undergoing momentous changes due to continuing migration from Latin America as well as a growing consciousness on the part of U.S. residents—Latina/o and non-Latina/o alike—of the importance of Latin American and Latina/o history and culture to the present and future of the Americas.[1]

In recent years Goldman has continued to write specifically from and about Mexico. From October 2014 through June 2015 he wrote a six-part series on the September 2014 disappearance of forty-three students from a teacher's school in Iguala, Guerrero, Mexico. The case was horrific because of the scale of the crime, and it contributed to the already rampant distrust of Mexican authorities. Goldman explained that the case "has come to stand for so many similar massacres and atrocities," including the massacre of forty-five indigenous people (mostly women and children) in Acteal, Chiapas, in December 1997, and the discovery of seventy-two murdered Central American migrants in the northern state of Tamaulipas in 2010.[2] Like the victims of those crimes, the students were members of a marginalized community: they came from poor, rural, and largely indigenous families. As he did in *The Interior Circuit*, Goldman has relayed information from Mexican blogs and reporters to his U.S. readers, offering his audience an insider's understanding of the crime. And like the kidnapping of a dozen people outside a club in Mexico City that he discussed in his 2014 *crónica,* this crime bears the mark of both narco-violence and government complicity. Goldman explained that the recovered corpse of one student bore the gruesome trademarks of a narco-murder. Immediately following the disappearance, the mayor of the town, José Luis Albarca, fled with his wife, whose brother is allegedly the leader of a narco-trafficking gang Guerreros Unidos (United Warriors), with which the mayor ruled over Iguala and which was responsible for the disappearance. The motive behind the disappearance remains unclear; perhaps the mayor was angered that the students, who were in the midst of participating in a protest, had interrupted the mayor's wife as she gave a speech, or perhaps they were targeted because they represented a more general leftist threat to the corrupt government. Goldman explained that "Mexicans know from experience that the motives behind acts of narco-state violence are often bewildering and senseless."[3]

The case has continued to erode faith in the Mexican government while further revealing significant human rights abuses in the country. In the course of the investigation into the students' disappearance, several mass graves of other victims have been discovered, pointing toward horrific levels of violence and government corruption. The attorney general, Jesús Murrillo Karam, gave an account of the crime that claimed that the students' bodies had been burned; scientists from the Universidad Nacional Autónoma de México (National Autonomous University of Mexico) argued that it was in fact physically impossible for a fire capable of incinerating forty-two bodies to have occurred in the space Murrillo claimed it did.[4] The government's account was bolstered by other impossible claims, including one by a gang member who confessed that he had approached the fire while it was burning to add more fuel. Goldman subtly points to the ludicrous nature of the idea that one could approach a roaring fire "as if approaching a barbecue pit"; of course anyone doing so "would have been incinerated instantly."[5] In his most recent report on the case, published on the one-year anniversary of the disappearance in September 2015, Goldman related findings from an Interdisciplinary Group of Independent Experts (known by the Spanish acronym GIEI), which includes experts from Chile, Colombia, Guatemala, and Spain. The GIEI, which was appointed by the Inter-American Court of Human Rights, produced a report that has historic ramifications; the investigation was the first time that Mexico allowed foreign authorities to intrude on its juridical territory, and it was also "the first time Mexicans had ever seen a real criminal investigation."[6] A new piece of information revealed in the report was that the gang charged with participating in the murder, Guerreros Unidos, had been known to utilize commercial buses to transport drugs (heroin and cocaine) from Mexico to the United

States. The students had been killed after commandeering several commercial buses to transport themselves to a protest (a common practice in Mexico). It is possible that the students had unknowingly taken a bus that contained drugs; this would explain why they were targeted. The exact role of and motivation behind the Mexican government, including local, state, and federal authorities, and their involvement in covering up the crime and hindering the investigation remain unclear, but the existence of the GIEI report means that investigations into the crime will continue, perhaps in international venues. These revelations regarding violence, cover-ups, and lies have repercussions for the United States as well because the United States funds the Mexican forces and recently, under President Obama, increased aid to Mexico that was specifically aimed at bolstering Mexican border patrol with the goal of apprehending and deporting Central American migrants before they reach the United States.

Given his Central American roots and location in Mexico, it is no surprise that some of Goldman's most recent writing has focused on the fate of Central Americans in both the United States and Mexico. Central Americans from countries such as Guatemala, Honduras, and El Salvador travel thousands of miles through Mexican territory as they attempt to reach the United States. Increasingly these migrants are not simply seeking greater economic opportunities but are fleeing rampant violence; many people flee after witnessing crimes, losing family members, or receiving direct threats. In 2013 Goldman wrote the foreword to the English-language version of Óscar Martínez's *The Beast: Riding the Rails and Dodging Narcos on the Migrant Trail*. Published in Spanish under the perhaps more descriptive title *Los migrantes que no importan* (The Migrants That Don't Matter), Martínez's book details the horrors that Central Americans traveling through Mexico face. He specifically followed migrants who ride on top of freight trains, known collectively as *la bestia* (the beast), as they dodge robbery, rape, beatings, and murder at the hands of petty criminals, gangs, and Mexican authorities. In his foreword Goldman placed the book within a hemispheric context, explaining that the book was written by a Mexican journalist who is the son of Salvadoran exiles. Martínez's personal experiences with political and gang violence, including his encounter with a homeland that he found, six years after the official conclusion of its civil war, "more violent than before," spurred him to go "where no other journalist from Mexico or elsewhere had gone," physically accompanying migrants on their journeys, often at great personal risk.[7] Speaking to audiences in both the United States and Mexico, Goldman has lamented that the fate of Central American migrants has been largely neglected by both countries. He has accused both countries of "indifference, moral mediocrity and fear" and has pointed to the stark silences on behalf of both nations regarding their complicity in the ongoing humanitarian crisis.[8] The United States, through its support for repressive governments during the civil wars in Central America throughout the 1980s, directly contributed to the destabilization of these current migrant-sending countries. Appropriate given his own investment in narrative and journalism, Goldman has spoken eloquently of the importance of journalism in combating such silence as well as giving voice to those whose stories and lives are ignored, diminished, and degraded.

While all his work portrays a deep empathy and a political skepticism becoming more and more rare, Goldman has been careful not to impose a particular political sensibility on his writing. In an interview with Daniel Peña he spoke about the responsibilities he has felt as a writer, as a novelist, and as a journalist. "The last thing I would ever want to do, for example, is write a novel that would appear to want to tell people what to think about the immigration debate, and I would never write a novel whose sole ambition was to give a 'positive' view of immigrants. (I'm for open borders, by the way—down with the nation state!)"[9] This statement illustrates Goldman's own strongly held positions while accurately reflecting the complexity with which he has treated political and social subjects in his writing.

His comment about open borders, while made in an off-hand remark, is nevertheless an apt description of his own approach to writing and publishing. Goldman is part of a strong and growing cohort of contemporary writers who are literally reorienting U.S. and Latin American literature and calling on readers to rethink the relationship between the two hemispheres' languages, literatures, histories, and cultures. At Trinity College he teaches a course entitled "The Latin American Novel in English and Spanish." Such a title calls into question the relationship between language and literature and between the two continents. In writing about Latin America (specifically Central America) from a transnational perspective but in the English language, Goldman has both reflected and foreshadowed the deep connections among the American continents. While his works stress that transnational exchanges between U.S. and Latin American writers, intellectuals, and politicians are nothing new, his own standing as a successful contemporary writer does suggest that these exchanges and connections are receiving widespread attention and appreciation. Goldman stands alongside other important U.S. Latina/o authors who refuse to "choose" a Latin American- or U.S.-based identity or career trajectory. In this he is joined by writers such as Daniel Alarcón, Junot Díaz, Angie Cruz, and others who write in English but engage in events and collaborations with writers from the United States and Latin America. Alarcón, a Peruvian American writer, and Díaz and Cruz, both Dominican American writers, join the Guatemalan American but Mexican-living Goldman to display the diversity of

U.S. Latina/o writers and in particular the important attention being given to writers who are not members of the most recognizable Latina/o communities (Mexican Americans, Puerto Ricans, and Cuban Americans). And while Goldman's success in both English and Spanish—he was recently the only English-language author included in a list of featured authors at the Guanajuato, Mexico, book fair—is notable, we should also consider his writing an important reflection of inter-American relations. His success in both languages and countries suggests that just as English-language literature can be considered Mexican, so too should Spanish-language texts (not to mention texts written in other languages) increasingly be considered part of the Américano canon.

NOTES

Chapter 1: Understanding Francisco Goldman

1. Cutolo, "Power of Place."

2. Coppedge, "Interview with Francisco Goldman."

3. Goldman, "Daniel, Dona Violeta, Democracy," 70.

4. Goldman, "Daniel, Dona Violeta, Democracy," 70, 74.

5. Coppedge, "Interview with Francisco Goldman."

6. Bach, "Francisco Goldman: Writing Astride Two Worlds," 16.

7. Pease, "Introduction: Re-mapping the Transnational Turn," 10, 14.

8. Templeton, "Becoming Transnational and Becoming Machinery in Francisco Goldman's *The Ordinary Seaman*," 271.

9. The term "double consciousness" was coined by W. E. B. DuBois in his 1903 work *The Souls of Black Folks*. The term captures the split identity that marks the experience of African Americans and other racial minorities—in which one is always simultaneously seeing one's self through one's own eyes and the eyes of others.

10. Goldman, "Moro Like Me," 66.

11. Anzaldúa, *Borderlands/La Frontera*, 101.

12. Coppedge, "Interview with Francisco Goldman."

13. Ibid.

14. Arias, "Central American-Americans," 170–71, 185.

15. Bach, "Francisco Goldman: Writing Astride Two Worlds," 17.

16. Goldman, *Long Night of White Chickens*, 19.

Chapter 2: Searching for Self and Confronting Impunity in *The Long Night of White Chickens*

1. Shawn, "Guatemala Noche," 90.

2. Casey, "Paranoids with Real Enemies," BR20.

3. Gräbner, "'But How to Speak of Such Things?'" 55.

4. Arias, "La psique interior de los guatemaltecos, las cuestiones del biculturalismo," 635.

5. Kerrigan, "Investigating Guatemala," 21.

6. The name means "the little quetzales," a reference to the quetzal bird, which is the national bird of Guatemala as well as the name of that country's currency.

7. Moya may also be an amalgamation of more than one reporter. In his review of the novel, Guatemalan author Victor Perera wrote that he recognizes Moya as "Julio Godoy, the dashing and brilliant young journalist who was forced to flee Guatemala after he exposed corruption in high places" ("Metaphor for Guatemala"). But in his

own account of this particular incident—avoiding being kidnapped by a death squad—Goldman said that he was with Jean-Marie Simon, a photojournalist who worked in Guatemala between 1980 and 1988.

8. Craft, "International Adoption as a Fictional Construct," 430.

9. Kerrigan, "Investigating Guatemala," 21.

10. Gräbner, "'But How to Speak of Such Things?'" 55.

11. Goldman, *Long Night of White Chickens,* 5–6.

12. Arias, "La psique interior," 634, author's translation.

13. Bach, "Francisco Goldman: Writing Astride Two Worlds," 16.

14. Coppedge, "Interview with Francisco Goldman."

15. Goldman, "Sad Tales of La Libertad de Prensa," 57–58.

16. Batres is likely based on Oscar Clemente Marroquín or his brother José Rubén Zamora Marroquín or both. They are grandsons of Guatemalan politician and newspaperman Clemente Marroquín Rojas, who founded the newspaper *La Hora.* Arias, "La psique interior de los guatemaltecos, las cuestiones del biculturalismo," suggested that *El Minuto* refers to Rojas's *La Hora,* of which Marroquín currently serves as the editor. Zamora began his career working for *La Hora* but has since founded two Guatemalan papers, *Siglo Veintiuno* and *El Periódico.* He has faced death threats, beatings, and kidnappings for his outspoken reporting on government corruption (Goldman, *Art of Political Murder,* 143).

17. Goldman, *Art of Political Murder,* 146.

18. Goldman, *Long Night of White Chickens,* 330–31.

19. Ryan, *John Sayles, Filmmaker,* 200.

20. Goldman, "Some Reflections on *Men with Guns.*"

21. Goldman, *Long Night of White Chickens,* 330; Goldman, "Some Reflections on *Men with Guns.*"

22. Goldman, *The Interior Circuit,* 154.

23. Ibid.

24. Goldman, *Art of Political Murder,* 145.

25. Goldman, "Some Reflections on *Men with Guns.*"

26. Ibid.

27. Schlesinger and Kinzer, *Bitter Fruit,* 76.

28. Goldman, *Art of Political Murder,* 14.

29. Perera, "Metaphor for Guatemala."

30. Kerrigan, "Investigating Guatemala," 21.

31. In 1982 José Efraín Ríos Montt, a general in the Guatemalan Army, overthrew Lucas García to become president of the country. Ríos Montt was overthrown by his defense minister a year later. In 2013 the former president was convicted of genocide and crimes against humanity; a Guatemalan court overturned the conviction in 2014. A retrial that began in 2015 was suspended, owing in part to his deteriorating health.

32. Perera, "Metaphor for Guatemala."

33. Zimmerman, "Woody Allen visita Guatemala," 652.

34. *Guatemala: Never Again!,* 38.

35. "Japanese Tourist Killed by Mob in Guatemala Market."

36. Rosenberg, "Burying the Kirkpatrick Doctrine."

37. Bach, "Francisco Goldman: Writing Astride Two Worlds," 17.

38. Knishes, associated with Jewish communities, are an eastern European snack,

consisting of a potato or meat-filled dough. *Chapín* is a slang term for a Guatemalan person; the truck's product notably references both sides of Rogerio's heritage.

39. Bach, "Francisco Goldman: Writing Astride Two Worlds," 16.

40. Ibid.

Chapter 3: Movement and Memory in *The Ordinary Seaman*

1. Harford Vargas, *Forms of Dictatorship*, 90.

2. Ibid.

3. Caminero-Santangelo, "Central Americans in the City," 178.

4. The crew adopts the term "los blacks" from Elias; Harford Vargas pointed out that the combination of English (blacks) and Spanish (los) evokes a hemispheric history of slavery.

5. Caminero-Santangelo, "Central Americans in the City," 181.

6. Houston, "Barely Afloat."

7. Steinberg, "Ordinary Seaman," 55.

8. Houston, "Barely Afloat."

9. Shemak, *Asylum Speakers*, 199.

10. Lazo, "Hemispheric American Novels," 1089.

11. Templeton, "Becoming Transnational and Becoming Machinery in Francisco Goldman's *The Ordinary Seaman*," 284.

12. DeGuzmán, *Buenas Noches, American Culture*, 174.

13. Gruesz, "Utopia Latina," 72.

14. Rodríguez, "Refugees of the South," 403.

15. Naimou, *Salvage Work*, 57.

16. Moody, "Land Ho! The Ordinary Seaman."

17. Naimou, *Salvage Work*, 55.

18. Ibid., 59–61.

19. Ibid., 92.

20. Harford Vargas, *Forms of Dictatorship*, 90.

21. Moody, "Land Ho! The Ordinary Seaman."

22. Templeton, "Becoming Transnational and Becoming Machinery in Francisco Goldman's *The Ordinary Seaman*," 283.

23. Caminero-Santangelo, "Central Americans in the City," 179.

24. Shemak, *Asylum Speakers*, 207.

25. Harford Vargas, *Forms of Dictatorship*, 102.

26. Lazo, "Hemispheric American Novels," 1086.

27. Templeton, "Becoming Transnational and Becoming Machinery in Francisco Goldman's *The Ordinary Seaman*," 271.

Chapter 4: A View of History from the Center

1. Goldman has mentioned that the historical Aparicio went by the nickname Panchita. The novel's use of the name Paquita draws attention to the fact that this is a fictional character (Allen, "Francisco Goldman"). In another interview he noted that "the contemporary Guatemalan state is the fruit of Justo Rufino's brutality" (Bach, "Francisco Goldman: Writing Astride Two Worlds," 19).

2. Allen, "Francisco Goldman."

3. Birnbaum, "Francisco Goldman."

4. Mars-Jones, "Problem Like María."
5. Quoted in Birnbaum, "Francisco Goldman."
6. Mars-Jones, "Problem Like María."
7. Vigil, "*Divine Husband* and the Creation of a Transamericana Subject," 197.
8. Birnbaum, "Francisco Goldman."
9. Ibid.
10. Ibid.
11. Goldman, "Mexico DF," 105.
12. Jaggi, "Mongrel River."
13. Siegel, "Divine Husband."
14. Rodríguez, "Genealogías Transnacionales Centroamericanas: De Máximo Soto Hall a Francisco Goldman," 253, 246.
15. Vigil, "*The Divine Husband* and the Creation of a Transamericana Subject," 198.
16. Vigil, "Judaism, Sexuality and the Nation in Francisco Goldman's *The Divine Husband*," 90.
17. Goldman, *Divine Husband*, 135.
18. Vigil, "*The Divine Husband* and the Creation of a Transamericana Subject," 93.
19. Ibid., 96.
20. Ibid., 91.

Chapter 5: Confronting the Legacy of Violence in *The Art of Political Murder*

1. Goldman, *Art of Political Murder*, 65.
2. Goldman, "Murder Comes for the Bishop," 60.
3. Goldman, *Art of Political Murder*, 38.
4. Goldman, "Murder Comes for the Bishop," 60.
5. Goldman, *Art of Political Murder*, 118
6. Of all the individuals and organizations involved, Goldman claimed the "true hero" and only "real professional" was the head of police investigations for MINUGUA, the Spaniard Rafael Guillamón (quoted in Viñas, "Unscripted: Francisco Goldman and #RenunciaYa").
7. The book's dedication reads: "*Por los que creyeron*. For the believers. And in memory of Darinel Domingo Montejo, José Mérida Escobar, Mama Lotti, and others unnamed."
8. Curiel, "Murder in Guatemala."
9. Carroll, "Military Mendacity."
10. Ibid.
11. Stanford, "Art of Political Murder."
12. Viñas, "First WOLA-Duke Book Prize Announced."
13. Vargas Llosa, "Quién mató al Obispo?"
14. As his surname indicates, he is related to the military men arrested—he is the stepson of Colonel Lima Estrada and half-brother of Captain Lima Oliva.
15. It is also possible, as another person testified, that the order was reversed and that the younger Lima had botched the operation and called in his father to help. Perhaps the operation was only meant to steal some papers from the parish, not murder Gerardi.
16. Vargas Llosa, "Quién mató al Obispo?"
17. Rohter, "Guatemala Amnesty Is Approved."
18. Ibid., 5.
19. Ibid., 87.

20. Payne, *Unsettling Accounts,* 2

21. Goldman, *Art of Political Murder,* 6.

22. Schlesinger and Kinzer, *Bitter Fruit.* Of course the UFC had been undervaluing the stated worth of their land. While the government offered them $627,572, the company demanded $15,854,849 (76).

23. In 2001, no doubt in an effort to distance itself from the negative connotations of the School of the Americas, the training ground was renamed the Western Hemisphere Institute for Security and Cooperation (WHINSEC).

24. "U.S. School of the Americas Cited by Guatemalan Truth Commission Report."

25. Peña, "Rumpus Interview with Francisco Goldman."

26. Galicia, "Dos involucrados en Caso Gerardi murieron de forma similar."

27. Ibid.

28. Ahmed and Malkin, "Otto Pérez Molina."

29. Viñas, "Unscripted: Francisco Goldman."

30. In the book Goldman explained that Pérez Molina may have been the person who recruited Chanax to spy for the G-2. But in his 2015 article, the author suggested Chanax omitted the general's name out of fear.

31. Viñas, "Unscripted: Francisco Goldman."

Chapter 6: Love, Loss, and Literature

1. To distinguish between the author and the protagonist of the novel, the former will be referred to as Goldman and the latter as Francisco.

2. Byock, "Francisco Goldman on 'Say Her Name.'"

3. Ibid.

4. *Radio Ambulante,* "Radio Ambulante in New York."

5. Connelly, "'Say Her Name.'"

6. Borghino, "Death Proves an Impressive Muse for Francisco Goldman."

7. Ibid.

8. Mason, "*Publisher's Weekly* talks with Francisco Goldman," 35.

9. Byock, "Francisco Goldman on 'Say Her Name.'"

10. Celayo, "Francisco Goldman: Say Her Name."

11. Goldman, *Say Her Name,* 1.

12. Byock, "Francisco Goldman on 'Say Her Name.'"

13. Romm, "Marriage's Tragic Early End."

14. In the novel Aura's mother is named Juanita.

15. Goldman, "Nothing Helps," 24.

16. Mason, "*Publisher's Weekly* talks with Francisco Goldman," 35.

17. Freud, "Mourning and Melancholia," 244.

18. Mason, "*Publisher's Weekly* Talks with Francisco Goldman," 35.

19. Byock, "Francisco Goldman on 'Say Her Name.'"

20. Ibid.

21. In his nonfiction chronicle, Goldman identified the author of this work, Nicolas José, as a poet and Aura's boyfriend when the two attended college (*The Interior Circuit: A Mexico City Chronicle.,* 35).

Chapter 7: Around Mexico

1. Goldman, "Nothing Helps," 25.

2. Harford Vargas and Hanna, "Transnational Forms," 65.

3. Riding, "Travels in a Maze in Mexico."
4. Rath, "Interior Circuit Meditates on Grief and Mexico City."
5. Ullin, "Ghosts among Us."
6. Ibid.
7. Alarcón, "What I Read This Year"; Martínez, "Endless Mourning."
8. Rath, "Interior Circuit Meditates on Grief and Mexico City."
9. Ibid.
10. Ibid.
11. Goldman, "Crisis in Mexico: The Case of the Missing Forty-Three."
12. Quintero, "Más de 500 años de cárcel."
13. The hashtag originated from an off-the-cuff remark by the Mexican attorney general Jesús Murrillo. Seeking to end a November 2014 press conference about the disappearance of forty-three students two months earlier, Murrillo said "Ya me cansé" ("Enough, I'm tired"). The populace used the phrase to signal their own exhaustion with government corruption and criminal complicity.

Conclusion

1. "Latin America" denotes those nations, cultures, and histories located in the southern Western Hemisphere, including South and Central America. "Latina/o" denotes the cultures, histories, and languages of Latin American peoples in the United States. Because of the U.S. annexation of Mexico at the conclusion of the Mexican American War (1846–48) as well as the acquisition of Puerto Rico at the conclusion of the Spanish American War (1898), we must recognize that not all Latina/o peoples can trace their history to a location *outside* the current territorial boundaries of the United States. At the same time the development of a unique and in some cases panethnic experience and identity in the United States necessitates the use of terms that distinguish experiences and identities based in the United States (Latina/o) from those based outside of it (Latin American).
2. Goldman, "Missing Forty-Three: The Government's Case Collapses."
3. Goldman, "Crisis in Mexico: The Case of the Missing Forty-Three."
4. Goldman, "Missing Forty-Three: The Government's Case Collapses."
5. Goldman, "Mexico's Missing Forty-Three: One Year, Many Lies, and a Theory That Might Make Sense."
6. Ibid.
7. Martínez, *Beast,* viii.
8. Ibid., xv.
9. Peña, "Rumpus Interview with Francisco Goldman."

BIBLIOGRAPHY

Works by Goldman

BOOK-LENGTH PUBLICATIONS

The Art of Political Murder: Who Killed the Bishop? New York: Grove, 2007.

The Divine Husband. New York: Grove, 2004.

The Interior Circuit: A Mexico City Chronicle. New York: Grove, 2014.

The Long Night of White Chickens. New York: Grove, 1992.

The Ordinary Seaman. New York: Grove, 1998.

Say Her Name. New York: Grove, 2011.

UNCOLLECTED WORKS

"The Children's Hour." *Harper's,* October 1, 1984, 69–74.

"Crisis in Mexico: The Case of the Missing Forty-Three." *New Yorker,* October 24, 2014. http://www.newyorker.com/news/news-desk/crisis-mexico-disappearance-forty-three (accessed February 25, 2017).

"Daniel, Dona Violeta, Democracy." *Harper's,* February 1, 1990, 70–78.

"From President to Prison: Otto Pérez Molina and a Day for Hope in Guatemala." *New Yorker,* September 4, 2015. http://www.newyorker.com/news/news-desk/from-president-to-prison-otto-perez-molina-and-a-day-for-hope-in-guatemala (accessed February 25, 2017).

"Guatemalan Death Masque." *Harper's,* January 1, 1986, 56–63.

"Lost in Another Honduras." *Harper's,* October 1, 1986, 49–57.

"Mexico DF." In *The Beacon Best of 2001: Great Writing by Women and Men of all Colors and Cultures,* edited by Junot Díaz. Boston: Beacon, 2001, 104–11.

"Mexico's Missing Forty-Three: One Year, Many Lies, and a Theory That Might Make Sense." *New Yorker,* September 30, 2015. http://www.newyorker.com/news/news-desk/mexicos-missing-forty-three-one-year-many-lies-and-a-theory-that-might-make-sense (accessed February 25, 2017).

"The Missing Forty-Three: The Government's Case Collapses." *New Yorker,* June 8, 2015. http://www.newyorker.com/news/news-desk/the-missing-forty-three-the-governments-case-collapses (accessed February 25, 2017).

"Moro Like Me." In *Half and Half: Writers on Growing Up Biracial and Bicultural,* edited by Claudine C. O'Hearn. New York: Pantheon Books: 1998, 49–70.

"Murder Comes for the Bishop." *New Yorker,* March 15, 1999, 60–77.

"Nothing Helps." *Virginia Quarterly Review* 90 (Winter 2014): 22–25.

"Sad Tales of La Libertad de Prensa." *Harper's,* August 1, 1988, 56–62.

"Some Reflections on *Men with Guns*." http://www.sonyclassics.com/menwithguns/reflections.html (accessed February 25, 2017).

"What Price Panama." *Harper's*, September 1, 1990, 71–78.

Works Cited

Ahmed, Azam, and Elisabeth Malkin. "Otto Pérez Molina of Guatemala Is Jailed Hours after Resigning Presidency." *New York Times*, September 3, 2015. http://www.nytimes.com/2015/09/04/world/americas/otto-perez-molina-guatemalan-president-resigns-amid-scandal.html (accessed February 25, 2017).

Alarcón, Daniel. "What I Read This Year." *Gawker Review of Books*, December 23, 2014. http://review.gawker.com/what-i-read-this-year-daniel-alarcon-1669443325 (accessed February 25, 2017).

Allen, Esther. "Francisco Goldman." *Bomb Magazine* 88 (Summer): 2004. http://bombmagazine.org/article/2665/francisco-goldman (accessed February 25, 2017).

Anzaldúa, Gloria. *Borderlands/La Frontera: The New Mestiza*. 3rd ed. San Francisco: Aunt Lute Books, 2007.

Arias, Arturo. "La psique interior de los guatemaltecos, las cuestiones del biculturalismo." *Mesoamérica* 34 (December 1997): 633–36.

———. "Central American-Americans: Invisibility, Power and Representation in the US Latino World." *Latino Studies* (March 200): 168–87.

Bach, Caleb. "Francisco Goldman: Writing Astride Two Worlds." *Americas*, July–August 2005, 14–19.

Birnbaum, Robert. "Francisco Goldman." *Identity Theory*, December 8, 2004. http://www.identitytheory.com/francisco-goldman/ (accessed February 25, 2017).

Borghino, José. "Death proves an impressive muse for Francisco Goldman," Australian. July 16, 2011. (accessed January 4, 2017).

Byock, Lila. "Francisco Goldman on 'Say Her Name.'" *Paris Review*, May 3, 2011. http://www.theparisreview.org/blog/2011/05/03/francisco-goldman-on-say-her-name/ (accessed February 25, 2017).

Caminero-Santangelo, Marta. "Central Americans in the City: Goldman, Tobar and the Question of Pan Ethnicity." *LIT: Literature, Interpretation, Theory* 20, no. 3 (2009): 173–95.

Carroll, Rory. "Military Mendacity." *Guardian*, February 22, 2008. https://www.theguardian.com/books/2008/feb/23/politics (accessed February 25, 2017).

Casey, Constance. "Paranoids with Real Enemies: The Long Night of White Chickens by Francisco Goldman." *New York Times*, August 16, 1992, BR20.

Celayo, Armando. "Francisco Goldman: Say Her Name." *World Literature Today* 85, no. 5 (September–October 2011): 59. https://www.worldliteraturetoday.org/2011/september/say-her-name-francisco-goldman (accessed February 25, 2017).

Connelly, Phoebe. "'Say Her Name': The Blaze of a Shortened, Ardent Life." NPR. April 12, 2011. http://www.npr.org/2011/07/14/135317809/say-her-name-the-blaze-of-a-shortened-ardent-life (accessed February 25, 2017).

Coppedge, Whit. "Interview with Francisco Goldman." *Pif Magazine*, May 1, 2000. http://www.pifmagazine.com/2000/05/interview-with-francisco-goldman/ (accessed February 25, 2017).

Craft, Linda J. 1996. "International Adoption as a Fictional Construct: Francisco Goldman's *The Long Night of White Chickens*." In *Romance Languages Annual*, edited by

Jeanette Beer, Patricia Hart, and Ben Lawton. West Lafayette, Ind.: Purdue Research Foundation, 430–35.

Curiel, Carolyn. "Murder in Guatemala." *New York Times*, September 30, 2007. http://www.nytimes.com/2007/09/30/books/review/Curiel-t.html (accessed February 25, 2017).

Cutolo, Ruby. "The Power of Place." *Publisher's Weekly*, June 9, 2014, 36–37. http://www.publishersweekly.com/pw/by-topic/authors/profiles/article/62763-the-power-of-place-francisco-goldman.html (accessed February 25, 2017).

DeGuzmán, María. *Buenas Noches, American Culture: Latina/o Aesthetics of Night*. Bloomington: Indiana University Press, 2012.

"First WOLA-Duke Book Prize Announced." July 23, 2008. https://www.wola.org/2008/07/first-wola-duke-book-award-winner-announced/ (accessed February 25, 2017).

Freud, Sigmund. "Mourning and Melancholia." In *The Standard Edition of the Complete Psychological Works of Sigmund Freud Vol. IX*, trans. James Strachey. London: Hogarth Books, 1953–74, 243–58.

Galicia, Néstor. "Dos involucrados en Caso Gerardi murieron de forma similar." *Prensa Libre*, July 18, 2016. http://www.prensalibre.com/hemeroteca/muerte-de-byron-lima-oliva-y-obdulio-villanueva (accessed February 25, 2017).

Gräbner, Cornelia. "'But How to Speak of Such Things?': Decolonial Love, the Coloniality of Gender and Political Struggle in Francisco Goldman's *The Long Night of White Chickens* (1992) and Jennifer Harbury's *Bridge of Courage* (1994) and *Searching for Everado* (1997)." *Journal of Iberian and Latin American Studies* 20, no. 1 (2014): 51–74.

Gruesz, Kirsten Silva. "Utopia Latina: *The Ordinary Seaman* in Extraordinary Times." *Modern Fiction Studies* 49, no. 1 (Spring 2003): 54–83.

Guatemala: Never Again! REMHI: Recovery of Historical Memory Project. Official Report of the Human Rights Office, Archdiocese of Guatemala. Orbis Books, 1999.

Harford Vargas, Jennifer. *Forms of Dictatorship: Power, Narrative and Authoritarianism in the Latina/o Novel*. New York: Oxford University Press, 2017.

Harford Vargas, Jennifer, and Monica Hanna. "Transnational Forms." In *Latino/a Literature in the Classroom: 21st Century Approaches to Teaching*, edited by Frederick Luis Aldama. Routledge, 2015, 64–77.

Houston, Robert. "Barely Afloat." *New York Times*, March 16, 1997. https://www.nytimes.com/books/97/03/16/reviews/970316.16houstot.html (accessed February 25, 2017).

Jaggi, Maya. "Mongrel River." *Guardian*, May 5, 2005. https://www.theguardian.com/books/2005/may/07/featuresreviews.guardianreview17 (accessed February 25, 2017).

"Japanese Tourist Killed by Mob in Guatemala Market." Reuters. April 30, 2000. http://www.latinamericanstudies.org/guatemala/japanese.htm (accessed February 25, 2017).

José, Nicolas. "Apuntes para no olvidar a Aura Estrada Curiel (1977–2005)." *Letras Libres*, April 24, 2012. http://www.letraslibres.com/mexico-espana/apuntes-no-olvidar-aura-estrada-curiel-1977-2007 (accessed February 25, 2017).

Kerrigan, Michael. "Investigating Guatemala." *Times Literary Supplement*, January 15, 1993, 21.

Lazo, Rodrigo. "Hemispheric American Novels." In *The Cambridge History of the*

American Novel, edited by Leonard Cassuto, Clare Virginia Eby, and Benjamin Reiss. Oxford: Cambridge University Press, 2011, 1084–95.

Mars-Jones, Adam. "A Problem Like María." *Guardian*, January 8, 2005. https://www.theguardian.com/books/2005/jan/09/fiction.features2 (accessed February 25, 2017).

Martínez, Óscar. *The Beast: Riding the Rails and Dodging the Narcos on the Migrant Trail*, trans. Daniela Maria Ugaz and John Washington. London: Verso, 2013.

Martínez, Rubén. "Endless Mourning: Rubén Martínez on Francisco Goldman." *Los Angeles Review of Books*, July 8, 2014. https://lareviewofbooks.org/article/endless-mourning-ruben-martinez-francisco-goldman/ (accessed February 25, 2017).

Mason, Kara. "*Publisher's Weekly* Talks with Francisco Goldman: The Prosecutor; Say Her Name." *Publisher's Weekly*, February 14, 2011, 35.

Men with Guns. Dir. John Sayles. Independent Film Channel. 1997.

Moody, Rick. "Land Ho! The Ordinary Seaman." *Los Angeles Times*, February 16, 1997. http://articles.latimes.com/1997–2–16/books/bk-29255_1_ordinary-seaman (accessed February 25, 2017).

Naimou, Angela. *Salvage Work: U.S. and Caribbean Literatures amid the Debris of Legal Personhood*. New York: Fordham University Press, 2015.

Ortiz, Dianna. *The Blindfold's Eyes: My Journey from Torture to Truth*. Maryknoll, N.Y.: 2004.

Payne, Leigh. *Unsettling Accounts: Neither Truth nor Reconciliation in Confessions of State Violence*. Durham, N.C.: Duke University Press, 2008.

Pease, Donald E. "Introduction: Re-mapping the Transnational Turn." In *Re-framing the Transnational Turn in American Studies*, edited by Winfried Fluck, Donald E. Pease, and John Carlos Rowe. Hanover, N.H.: Dartmouth College Press, 2011. p. 10–49.

Peña, Daniel. "The Rumpus Interview with Francisco Goldman." October 26, 2015. http://therumpus.net/2015/10/the-rumpus-interview-with-francisco-goldman/ (accessed February 25, 2017).

Perera, Victor. "A Metaphor for Guatemala: The Long Night of White Chickens." Book review. *Los Angeles Times*, July 19, 1992. http://articles.latimes.com/1992–7–19/books/bk-4382_1_long-night-of-white-chickens (accessed February 25, 2017).

Quintero, Josefina. "Más de 500 años de cárcel para implicados en caso Heaven." *La Jornada*, July 23, 2016. http://www.jornada.unam.mx/ultimas/2016/07/23/mas-500-anos-de-carcel-para-implicados-en-caso-heaven (accessed February 25, 2017).

Radio Ambulante. "Radio Ambulante in New York." 2013. http://radioambulante.org/en/blog-en/ra-new-york (accessed February 25, 2017).

Rath, Arun. "'The Interior Circuit' Meditates on Grief and Mexico City." *Weekend Edition Sunday*, National Public Radio. July 13, 2014. http://www.npr.org/2014/07/13/331133763/the-interior-circuit-is-a-meditation-on-grief (accessed February 25, 2017).

Riding, Alan. "Travels in a Maze in Mexico." *New York Times*, July 23, 2014. https://www.nytimes.com/2014/07/24/books/the-interior-circuit-by-francisco-goldman.html (accessed February 25, 2017).

Robinson, Roxana. "Francisco Goldman's 'Say Her Name.'" *Washington Post*, April 14, 2011. https://www.washingtonpost.com/entertainment/books/book-review-francisco-goldmans-say-her-name/2011/03/22/AFGTz5eD_story.html (accessed February 25, 2017).

Rodríguez, Ana Patricia. "Genealogías Transnacionales Centroamericanas: De Máximo Soto Hall a Francisco Goldman." *Revista Iberoamericana* 79, no. 242 (January–March 2013): 243–56.

———. "Refugees of the South: Central Americans in the US Latino Imaginary." *American Literature* 73, no. 2 (2001): 387–412.

Rohter, Larry. "Guatemalan Amnesty Is Approved over Opponents' Objections." *New York Times,* December 19, 1996. http://www.nytimes.com/1996/12/19/world/guatemalan-amnesty-is-approved-over-opponents-objections.html (accessed February 25, 2017).

Romm, Robin. "A Marriage's Tragic Early End." *New York Times Sunday Book Review,* April 7, 2011. http://www.nytimes.com/2011/04/10/books/review/book-review-say-her-name-by-francisco-goldman.html (accessed February 25, 2017).

Rosenberg, Scott. "Burying the Kirkpatrick Doctrine." *Salon,* December 8, 2006. http://www.salon.com/2006/12/08/kirkpatrick_2/ (25 February 2017).

Ryan, Jack. *John Sayles, Filmmaker: A Critical Study and Filmography.* 2nd ed. Jefferson, N.C.: McFarland, 2010.

Schlesinger, Stephen C., and Stephen Kinzer. *Bitter Fruit: The Story of the American Coup in Guatemala.* Cambridge, Mass.: David Rockefeller Center for Latin American Studies, 2005.

Shawn, Wallace. "Guatemala Noche: A Conversation with Francisco Goldman." *Village Voice,* July 21, 1992, 90–93.

Shemak, April. *Asylum Speakers: Caribbean Refugees and Testimonial Discourse.* New York: Fordham University Press, 2011.

Siegel, Lee. "'The Divine Husband': Grand Illusions." *New York Times,* September 26, 2004. http://www.nytimes.com/2004/09/26/books/review/the-divine-husband-grand-illusions.html?_r=0 (accessed February 25, 2017).

Stanford, Peter. "The Art of Political Murder: Who Killed Bishop Gerardi? By Francisco Goldman." *Independent,* March 15, 2008. http://www.independent.co.uk/arts-entertainment/books/reviews/the-art-of-political-murder-who-killed-bishop-gerardi-by-francisco-goldman-795533.html (accessed February 25, 2017).

Steinberg, Sybil S. "The Ordinary Seaman." *Publishers Weekly* 243, no. 38 (November 25, 1996): 55.

Templeton, Michael. "Becoming Transnational and Becoming Machinery in Francisco Goldman's *The Ordinary Seaman.*" *Symploke* 14, no. 1–2 (2006): 271–88.

Ullin, David L. "Ghosts among Us: Francisco Goldman Maps His Haunted Life and His Place in Mexico City." *Los Angeles Times,* July 6, 2014, E1.

"U.S. School of the Americas Cited by Guatemalan Truth Commission Report." *SOAW.* http://www.soaw.org/news/news-alerts/3179 (accessed February 25, 2017).

Vargas Llosa, Mario. "Quién mató al Obispo?" *El País,* February 22, 2004. http://elpais.com/diario/2004/02/22/opinion/1077404405_850215.html (accessed February 25, 2017).

Vigil, Ariana. "*The Divine Husband* and the Creation of a Transamericana Subject." *Latino Studies* 11, no. 2 (Summer 2013): 190–207.

———. "Judaism, Sexuality, and the Nation in Francisco Goldman's *The Divine Husband.*" In *Returning to Babel: Jewish Latin American Representations and Experiences,* edited by Amalia Ran and Jean Cahan. Boston: Brill, 2012, 89–102.

———. "Unscripted: Francisco Goldman." *Radio Ambulante.* October 9, 2015. http://

radioambulante.org/en/audio-en/unscripted-francisco-goldman-y-renunciaya (February 25, 2017).

Zimmerman, Marc. "Woody Allen visita Guatemala: O una reivindicación frustrada; Consideraciones sobre la novela de Francisco Goldman." *Mesoamérica* 34 (December 1997): 651–66.

INDEX